School Focused Staff Development

Guidelines for Policy Makers

School Focused Staff Development

Guidelines for Policy Makers

Eric Hewton

 The Falmer Press

(A member of the Taylor & Francis Group)
London • New York • Philadelphia

UK   The Falmer Press, Falmer House, Barcombe, Lewes, East Sussex, BN8 5DL

USA   The Falmer Press, Taylor & Francis Inc., 242 Cherry Street, Philadelphia, PA 19106-1906

First published 1988

Library of Congress Cataloging in Publication Data

Hewton, Eric.
  School focused staff development.

  Bibliography: p.
  Includes index.
  1. Teachers—In-service training—Great Britain.
2. Careers development—Great Britain. 3. School
personnel management—Great Britain. I. Title.
LB1731.H45 1988 371.1′46′0941 87-33072
ISBN 1-85000-273-8
ISBN 1-85000-274-6 (pbk.)

Jacket design by Caroline Archer

Typeset in 11/13 Bembo by
Imago Publishing Ltd, Thame, Oxon

Printed in Great Britain by Taylor & Francis (Printers) Ltd, Basingstoke

Contents

This book is based on research funded by the Economic and Social Research Council (ESRC) reference number C00232202

Preface

In January 1986 I visited a comprehensive school in East Sussex and talked to several teachers about a staff development policy recently introduced by the school. I heard about (i) an introductory programme for student and probationary teachers; (ii) 'being a pupil for a day' and attending all lessons to understand better the routine from a pupil's point of view; (iii) a new scheme for giving teachers experience of some of the jobs they might face at a later stage in their career such as timetabling, chairing committees or organizing examinations; (iv) short in-house courses on computers and on improving tutorial skills; (v) various working parties on curriculum or other areas of concern at the time; (vi) a series of visits by teachers to other schools and industrial organizations and (vii) an embryo appraisal scheme that several senior staff had tried on a voluntary basis.

There was little doubt that those I spoke to were excited about the new opportunities for staff development. Somehow, the message that greater control over their own programme of activities was something that could benefit the teachers and the school, in an otherwise pretty bleak period, had reached many members of staff.

A few days later I found similar situations in two primary schools. Here the activities were quite different. In one I learned that several teachers had formed pairs or groups of three and were engaged in an ongoing scheme of mutual classroom observation. In the other, I learned that all teachers were in the process of renegotiating job descriptions with the head. In both schools, the staff were becoming accustomed to visiting other schools in order to witness alternative ways of teaching. Again, as in the secondary school, there was noticable enthusiasm for the outcomes of the staff development policy.

The schools were part of a pilot scheme which had started a year earlier. The scheme stemmed from a collaborative project between

East Sussex County Council and the University of Sussex which was concerned with INSET planning in the LEA and its schools. There was, and still is, considerable interest by central government, the DES and many LEAs in the importance of policy, signifying planning and greater control over programmes and resources. There had also been a general shift in thinking about INSET as a mainly external course activity to something that schools did, at least partly, for themselves. These two ideas — policy making and school-focussed staff development — formed the basis for a proposal submitted to the Economic and Social Research Council (ESRC). The proposal was accepted and a grant was awarded which enabled the project to begin in April 1985.

The project was unusual, although not exceptional, in so far as it was jointly planned and organized by a university and an LEA. There were two directors, Bob Garner, an adviser for the county (later to become County Adviser for School-Focussed Staff Development) and myself, a Reader in Education at the University. We appointed a Project Coordinator for a year, Tony Ward, a deputy head of an East Sussex comprehensive school not then involved in the project. At the end of that time he was replaced by a coordinator/evaluator, Paul Walsh, a head of house from a Brighton comprehensive school.

The project was called School-Focussed Staff Development or SFSD (the optional spelling of 'focussed' rather than 'focused' being preferred). Seven schools joined the project initially and each was represented by one person seconded to the project, full-time, for a term. They were called teacher-fellows because their secondment was funded under a DES scheme which attached that title to teachers attending the University. The directors, coordinator, evaluator and teacher fellows formed the project team.

By September 1985 the pilot schools had prepared their policies and had begun to put them into effect. In January 1986 I was making visits to the schools of the kind described above. But not all the information I received was as positive as that mentioned earlier: there were problems too. These proved as important as the successes in understanding the nature of SFSD. From both, the team learned a great deal about the meaning of staff development, the process of innovation, resistance to change and policy making.

This book is about such matters. It is not the first book to be written about school-focussed or school-based staff development and the literature will be referred to in later chapters. Two schemes, however, deserve special mention here. The SITE (Schools and In-Service Teacher Education) project was one of the first to pioneer a school-focussed scheme and the Sussex team were helped by the materials which were produced describing their work and its wider implications (for example, Davies, 1981; Baker 1982; and Northamptonshire LEA, 1984). The Schools Council book on school-based staff development activities (Oldroyd, Smith and Lee, 1984) was also of considerable value, particularly the many examples of ideas that had been tried in the schools associated with that project.

So, why another book on the subject? As we moved into our work in East Sussex we quickly realized the complexity of the task we were undertaking. What seemed from a distance to be a fairly straightforward exercise soon became enmeshed in a whole range of conceptual, managerial, political and financial problems. As we began to unravel them a number of questions arose. What is a policy and what should it contain? How wide a range of activities should a school be responsible for under its own policy? How should schemes be introduced into schools? How should needs for staff development be ascertained? What would be the resource implications of SFSD and how should the matter of costs be dealt with? How would the growing interest in, and concern about appraisal, fit in with the notion of SFSD? Would policies affect relationships and traditional ways of making decisions about INSET? Might this lead to conflict? And, finally what part should the County play in encouraging, supporting and financing SFSD?

All of these issues are dealt with in the forthcoming chapters. Where the book differs from its predecessors is in its contribution to the discussion of needs analysis, the nature of policies, the process of policy making and the role of the LEA in connection with SFSD. *It is written primarily for those schools wishing to prepare and implement school-focussed staff development policies and for LEAs that are moving towards an overall policy in this respect.* Although drawing upon the experience of primary and secondary schools, most of the ideas and lessons are equally applicable to colleges of further education. Those interested in staff-development generally will also find it of value, particularly the sections on needs assessment and staff development policies.

The book is in three parts. Part 1 looks first at the changing nature of INSET and staff development and then at the SFSD project and its outcomes. Part 2 draws upon the experience of the project and presents ideas about needs for staff development and how to go about assessing them. Part 3 deals with a number of matters of immediate concern to the policy maker. These include; the importance and nature of policies, what they might contain, examples of policies and finally the wider implications of SFSD for planning and providing INSET at county level.

A substantial part of this book was written between January and May 1987. During that time the events associated with the dispute over teachers' pay, conditions and negotiating rights were moving very fast indeed. The book is about school-focussed staff development and much of what is said remains true whatever the political and economic climate. But there is little point in pretending that national events, and particularly the long running dispute, have not affected the attitudes of teachers to the scheme which is described here and the extent to which implementation of plans has been possible.

These matters are mentioned throughout the book but the situation is changing almost week by week. Many outstanding issues remain to be clarified. For instance, the document *School Teachers' Pay and Conditions of Employment: The Government's Proposals* was published in March 1987. There was subsequently some 'consultation' and amendments. In April 1987 the proposals became law but they will not be implemented until September. During the summer, LEAs and teachers' associations will be attempting to establish exactly what the new conditions will mean in practice. What the future outcomes of the continuing dispute will be also remain uncertain and the effect of the government's general election success on negotiations can only be anticipated.

From the point of view of someone writing about staff development at this time there are many unanswered questions which may affect the implementation and progress of the SFSD scheme described. The following are some of the questions which may or may not be answered before publication. To what extent will consultation, negotiations, discussions, bargaining etc still continue with respect to the terms and conditions contained in the above mentioned document? What will happen when the implementation date arrives in September 1987? What will be the effect of the appraisal conditions? Will there be an attempt to implement them or will this have to await the outcome of the national pilot schemes? Will time for appraisal count as part of the 1265 hours of work referred to in the pay and conditions document? Will the five non-teaching days be used for INSET? What will be the effect of the rules concerning cover and how will this affect a school that wishes to obtain supply cover in order to release a teacher for less than two days to engage in staff development activities? These and many more issues will continue to exercise teachers and their associations, administrators and politicians over the coming months or years.

The dispute which began over pay and conditions has now extended to the loss of negotiating rights. Different teachers' associations take different attitudes as to what is on offer, whether or not to accept it in total or in part and what further action should be taken. The matter is highly complex and rapidly changing. In refering to these problems from time to time in connection with SFSD and appraisal the short phrase 'industrial dispute' will be used to cover the whole area of concern, conflict and action over pay, conditions and negotiating rights and any action that might be taken by the parties concerned in support of their stance. This form of 'shorthand' is intended to avoid distraction from the main message of the book which is concerned with the benefits that might be obtained from school-focussed staff development.

In working through and implementing the project's philosophy and putting together these chapters I must thank, particularly, Bob Garner and Tony Ward for their constant interest, endeavour and imaginative ideas. Also my thanks to the teacher fellows from the pilot schools. Theirs was the difficult task of convincing colleagues of the value of SFSD and getting it going at a very difficult time. Also my gratitude to Paul Walsh who had to pick up the threads in order to make sense of the evaluation. Finally, my thanks to those who read all or part of the draft manuscript and, apart from those already mentioned above, I would like to include Michael Eraut and Peter North. I hope what follows does justice to them all.

Part I
School-focussed Staff Development (SFSD): A Pilot Project and its Outcome

School-focussed staff development is described and analyzed conceptually and in practice. The gradual shift in emphasis from external, course-based IN-SET to school-based and school-focussed provision is traced and explained. The rationale behind the East Sussex SFSD project is examined and the outcomes of the scheme over two years are discussed. The role of the LEA in supporting and coordinating SFSD is examined.

1 SFSD and its Context

There is no doubt that education and schools are changing and, alongside these changes, the whole nature of the in-service education and training of teachers (INSET) is changing too. We need to consider what has, and is, happening in order to appreciate the origins and nature of School-Focussed Staff Development. I will, first, deal briefly with some of the major changes in education in recent years and then look at some the reasons which have underpinned the considerable reformulation of ideas and attitudes to do with INSET and staff development.

Changes in Education and the Effect upon Schools

A number of important events have occurred in the last fifteen years which have brought about substantial changes in the education system. These, in their turn, have contributed to changes in the nature and purpose of INSET. First, education has suffered a loss of prestige in the eyes of the Government and the public. There are many complex reasons for this. Much faith was placed in education to correct social and economic problems and this faith was used to justify steadily increasing expenditure over three decades since the last war. But the expected outcomes did not materialize and, if anything, problems became worse. It mattered little to the critics that the expectations were probably too high and that there were many other causes for the apparent lack of success. For them, state education was failing and the expenditure was not justified. Education thus suffered a blow to its prestige.

Partly as a result of this and partly because successive governments attempted to control public expenditure, education moved from a period of sustained financial growth to one of contraction. Those involved in providing the service can offer considerable evidence of the slow but steady decline in available resources since the mid 1970s (Hewton, 1986). The state of buildings and the shortages of materials and equipment are there for all to see.

It is difficult to disentangle the effects of falling rolls from the financial constraints but it is not difficult to see the results. First, primary and then secondary schools have had smaller numbers of pupils to deal with (although recently there has been an upturn in those entering the primary sector). Teachers have been shed, largely through early retirement and many schools have been closed or amalgamated with others. In this contracting situation there have been fewer opportunities to move or gain promotion. Many teachers have felt trapped and frustrated.

If the three factors — prestige, financial contraction and falling roles — are combined there emerges a picture of a state system which is, at best, struggling and, at worst, failing to respond adequately to the many new demands being placed upon it. A single quote from an HMI report (1982) sums up the situation.

> At the time of their visits to institutions, HMI gained the impression of continued professional commitment and resourcefulness but of the teachers' morale worn very thin as the uncertainties and changes arising from falling rolls and cuts in expenditure affect both the maintenance of present standards and attempts to bring about improvements. For many LEA officers and teachers a particular frustration is that of being unable, because of shortages of funds and resources and tight controls on staffing, to capitalize on the benefits that could arise from the fall in pupil numbers or to respond to problems or new needs of which both officers and teachers are acutely aware. (p. 13)

The problems and new needs referred to in this statement have accompanied a decade of extensive curriculum and organizational change. Most of the changes were important and necessary, but they have often been imposed and adopted with little consultation, within a very limited timescale and, for the most part, with only meagre resources to assist planning and implementation. Some of the changes which have important implication for teaching, learning and school management are listed below. Some affect all schools, others apply to either primary or secondary schools.

There have been demands to produce aims and objectives, curriculum statements and school self-evaluation reports; requirements to cater for children with special needs following the 1981 Education Act; the expectation that new technologies would be assimilated into curriculum and management practices.

There have been curriculum developments in many subject areas, particularly the teaching of maths, science and CDT. New assessment procedures including profiling, records of achievement and standardized tests have been introduced. Secondary schools have been expected to improve their practices in relation to pastoral care, and to introduce teaching regarding health-related fitness, sex education and equality plus a whole range of pre-vocational courses as well as the new GCSE, with all the changes which that requires in curriculum planning, teaching methods and assessment. The idea of a modular and integrated approach to the curriculum has been strongly encouraged. DES Circular 6/84 has set up a system whereby many 'activities which appear to the Secretary of State to be of importance' should be initiated by LEAs and schools and supported by specific grants.

The management of schools has received particular attention. Changes in decision making structures have been encouraged or required in order to accommodate more staff participation; improved team building has been expected; more community and parental involvement has been required; new governing bodies have been appointed with greater powers and some LEAs have expected schools to accept much greater autonomy in managing their own financial affairs. More recently, the debate about appraisal has consolidated itself within a whole new set of proposed (and controversial) working conditions and responsibilities associated with a reconstituted pay structure (DES, 1987), and, coming soon, a 'National Curriculum'.

The list is far from exhaustive and might easily be extended with each school and each LEA adding changes which have effected them in their own particular circumstances. A case for radically different forms of INSET provision can clearly be made to help deal with many of these changes.

The INSET Response

It is not the intention here to trace the history of INSET nor to analyze its nature and possible styles. The former has been well documented by Henderson (1981) and the latter by Eraut (1985). A brief resume will suffice for present purposes. Henderson suggests some of the limitations of the traditional INSET external, course-based approach.

> First, there was all too often a mismatch between the needs of teachers (whether personal needs or those arising from the school context in which they were working) and the content of courses. Such mismatch arose partly from inadequate analysis or understanding of the problems by course organizers, partly from inadequate description of course content in advertising material, and partly from the unsystematic way in which teachers selected courses. It also arose partly from the heterogeneous course membership. Second, even when a mismatch did not occur, and a course was of potential value to the participants, they were often unable to utilize new knowledge and skills acquired on the course because they were unable to influence what was happening in their schools, whether for reasons of status, lack of resources, lack of appropriate feedback mechanisms from the course to the schools, or some combination of these.
>
> ...Courses might serve some useful functions, but alternative forms of INSET provision had to be found to enable teachers and schools to respond to, control and direct their changing circumstances. (p. 8)

These changing circumstances are considerable as already pointed out. They require schools to adapt to reduced financial provision, falling rolls, major curriculum innovations, new technologies, alternative organization and management approaches and demands for reviews, evaluations and accountability — all against a background of a long running pay and conditions dispute and a general problem of lowered morale.

Eraut (1985) locates INSET arising from this situation within what he calls the 'change paradigm' in which 'the rationale is based on the need for the educational system to keep abreast of, if not anticipate, changes in wider society; and for schools to relate to changes in their local community'. But he contrasts the 'change paradigm', which is largely associated with external stimuli, with the 'problem solving paradigm'. This he argues:

> assumes that, because education is an inherently difficult and complex process and because circumstances are constantly changing, problems will inevitably arise in individual schools

and classrooms. These problems are best diagnosed by the teachers most closely concerned because only they know the students and the context sufficiently well. INSET activities should be closely geared to the study and solution of these problems. (p. 2514).

Schools and colleges are thus pressured from two sources ; from external change and from internal problems. It seems reasonable and logical, therefore, that they should be accorded a much greater say in the 'what' and 'how' of INSET provision. One model, already being advocated in the 1970s and aimed at providing greater internal control, was school-based INSET. It was suggested by those who had tried or wished to try this approach that a school, acting as a learning community, could identify and solve many of its problems including the INSET needs of its staff. The school would, if sufficiently motivated by a greater sense of control and direction over its own affairs, find the resources to provide INSET activities according to its own particular needs.

But there were limitations to this approach. One was a danger of parochialism. It was recognized that teachers had much to learn from other schools and those providing training in other institutions. Also, the range of activities which could be provided by the schools themselves was limited by resources, particularly in the smaller ones. Further, there was the danger that schools might concentrate on what they perceived to be their own internal problems and overlook changing external circumstances. Finally, the question was asked who was INSET for — the teachers or the school? There was always the possibility that the current needs of the school as an institution might override the personal and professional needs of the individual teacher.

It was with these problems and these questions in mind that the notion of school-*focussed* INSET began to appear. INSET provision should, surely, make use of both internal and external expertise and resources. The school should provide the focus for the identification of needs but the location of INSET activities associated with these needs should take place wherever it seemed most appropriate.

Perry (1977), in an often quoted statement, defined school-focussed INSET as: 'all the strategies employed by trainers and teachers in partnership to direct training programmes in such a way as to meet the identified needs of the school, and to raise the standards of teaching and learning in the classroom'.

It is assumed that the needs of the school in this definition include those of the teacher as well. As the idea of school-focussed INSET

7

was developed through pilot schemes, such as the SITE project (involving about fifty schools in four LEAs) the school itself increasingly became the focus for planning and direction and in many cases drew up a programme of activities which required input from outside agencies. Baker (1980) sets out certain principles of school-focussed INSET as developed by the SITE project and the first three are as follows:

1 that the schools should engage in a needs analysis to determine the INSET requirements of staff by whatever means they considered appropriate;
2 that these requirements should be put in order of priority and formulated into a programme of suggestions for INSET activities...
3 that the programme was to be given to a project coordinator or external 'linkage agent', who would commence negotiations to find a suitable provider and facilitate contact between the provider and school. (p. 182)

The model which emerged from this was of schools identifying their own needs for INSET and negotiating with outside agencies to provide for those needs. This raises a number of questions. What kind of needs should be included? Whose needs are they? How are they ascertained? How are they put into priority order? How is the programme drawn up? And, to what extent should schools be involved in satisfying their own needs? These were all questions which concerned those following on from the earlier work of the SITE team and they have been central to the evolution of SFSD.

School-Focussed Staff Development

The first point to consider is the significance of the term staff development rather than INSET. To some extent it is a matter of preference and the two terms are used by many writers interchangably. Hoyle (1972), for instance, suggested that INSET should should be linked to specific innovations, that INSET should focus upon functioning groups such as departmental teams but that schools should establish their own *staff development* policies.

Morant (1981), discussing the 'school-focused approach' to in-service education comments: 'As the institutional requirements of the school determine reference points for staff development, the teachers should assume collective responsibility for analysing pro-fessional needs...'. The Advisory Committee for the Supply and Education of Teachers (ACSET,1983), comments, in relation to school-based INSET, that training should be provided for heads and other senior members of staff as promotors or supporters of staff development.

So, is there a difference between the terms? The literature on the subject is of no great help in distinguishing between the two. Although, at first sight, development might appear to be a broader concept it is possible to find definitions of INSET which are equally comprehensive. If, for instance, Eraut's (1985) categories of INSET activities are accepted it is hard to envisage how development might extend beyond these. The categories are:

(i) *Job-embedded.* The emphasis is on actual performance in the classroom. Analysis of television tapes of one's teaching is given as an example.

(ii) *Job-related.* The training does not take place whilst teaching is going on, for example a group of teachers in an after school workshop on team-teaching.

(iii) *General professional.* Experience to improve or extend gener-al competence. The example quoted is of science teachers participating in workshops on the teaching of biology.

(iv) *Career/credential.* Education or training to obtain a quali-fication or prepare for a new role.

(v) *Personal.* Any course or experience which might facilitate personal development and may or may not be job-related.

This is a comprehensive list and it seems likely that most teachers would find their broadest developmental needs covered by these cate-gories. So if INSET and staff development do differ it is more likely to involve the term 'staff'. 'In-service education and training' (INSET) is normally accompanied by the words 'of teachers': it is the teacher who is being educated or trained. 'Staff development', however, is concerned with 'staff' and this can be taken to mean both the indi-viduals and the collectivity of teachers who together form the main workforce of the school. Staff development, therefore, is concerned with both the needs of individuals and those of the organization as a whole. What this means in practice is dealt with in chapters 3 and 4 but, for the present, it is suggested that the use of the term staff development opens up the possibility of a much wider range of activities than would seem to be implied by the in-service education and training of teachers. The whole school or the various functional sub-units within it also become targets for development. This was an assumption that underpinned the SFSD project.

The SFSD Project: A Response to Change

The proposal submitted to the Economic and Social Research Council in 1984 on behalf of East Sussex County Council and the University of Sussex contained many of the points referred above but it extended the area of interest to include the problem of policy making at both school and LEA level. The following extract summarizes the main thrust of the proposal.

> It is clear that INSET, and more specifically School-Focussed Staff Development, have already received a considerable amount of attention and experimentation. The lessons learned, particularly in relation to the value of problem solving and consultancy approaches. the need for organization development and the applicability of management development practices in the industrial and commercial field, must form an essential platform from which to move forward. But there is a further important, as yet relatively unexplored, aspect of the problem which this project will attend to. This relates to policy making at both school and county level and the implementation of such policies using realistic and carefully phased targets to bring about desired developments... Staff development must, therefore, be closely integrated with policy review and development and equip the school and its teachers to respond speedily and positively to meet the rapidly changing socio-economic and technical demands of the 1980's...
>
> It is the intention of the local authority to develop a framework for the county relating to school-focussed staff development. Within this framework schools will be encouraged and supported in developing their own school-focussed staff development schemes. The Authority will also seek to maximize the use of available resources to maintain such a scheme.

Policy and a more coordinated and integrated approach to INSET and staff development planning at school and LEA level were to be the hallmarks of the project. It was planned in two stages. Stage 1 would be devoted to drawing up and implementing staff development policies in seven pilot schools and stage 2, a year later, would continue this process and move towards the formulation of county policy regarding SFSD.

School Policies

An attempt was made to choose schools which varied in the extent of their existing involvement in staff development. some of those asked were known to be active in this field but others were less so or not at all. The selection procedure was also intended to produce a group of schools which would provide a contrast in terms of size, location and management style. The heads of seven schools eventually selected, all expressed keen interest in SFSD although it is doubtful whether more than one or two had much idea of its meaning and implications and, as was to emerge later, the degree of commitment varied somewhat.

The seven schools included three comprehensives (the smallest with 700 pupils and the largest with 1200) and four primary schools (ranging from 300 to 500 pupils). One secondary school was represented by its head and the other two by a deputy head. There was a head, a deputy head, a senior mistress and a scale 2 teacher from the primary schools. All seven 'teacher fellows', as they were called, were seconded for a term and spent their time partly at the University and partly in their own school.

The main purpose of the exercise was to find out what was involved in producing school policies and what advantages there would be in so doing. In a newsletter (sent to all schools in the County for information) the aims of the scheme were set out. It was indicated that each school involved should:

(i) Consider its requirements in the area of staff development and devise a realistic policy and the procedures for its implementation.
(ii) Assess carefully the resources available for implementing the policy and use these to optimum advantage.
(iii) Assist teachers to continue and enhance their professional development.
(iv) Ensure that all of these benefit pupils and improve their education.

The preferred approach for drawing up policy statements in the schools was set out in the ESRC proposal.

Although the method of working towards policies and programmes will be a matter for negotiation with each school some possibilities can be suggested in advance.

(a) The approach envisaged will be participative, involving as many members of staff as possible. The exercise, in itself, might be regarded as part of the staff development programme.

(b) The following formal aspects of staff development should be given particular attention:

  (i) the need for clearly-stated institutional and departmental policies for staff development;

  (ii) the specification of roles and structures within the school allocating particular responsibility for policy implementation. In other words — who will do what for whom and with what authority?

The schools began the task of producing a policy for school-focussed staff development in April 1985. Their policy documents were to be completed by July for implemention in September. The full implementation of the policies was delayed by the industrial action but despite this, all of the schools were able to implement some of the programmes scheduled for autumn 1985 and spring and summer 1986. Further parts of the programme were implemented in the following year. The policies provided a means of coordinating existing activities (which some schools had engaged in for some time) with new initiatives which had sometimes been discussed within the school but not carried further. Details of the programmes and activities undertaken by the schools are included in chapter 2.

All schools were required to cost their programmes before receiving funding from the Authority to carry out those activities which they could not otherwise afford. The Authority agreed to make available the equivalent of one day supply cover per teacher per school for the year with a minimum of £500 for primary schools and a maximum of £5000 for secondary schools. This was not an entitlement nor a budget. Rather it represented the maximum amount that could be bid for on the basis of an analysis of staff development needs and a written policy statement indicating how these needs would be met. The costed policy statements were first to be approved at County Hall and then money could be claimed against the agreed sum as and when necessary. The money available was to cover only school-based activities and visits. Other courses normally provided by the County (at teacher's centres or by the advisory service for instance) or courses offered by regional or national training institutions would be mentioned in the policies but would continue to be separately funded.

Policy at County Level

By the end of the first year it was decided to extend the project in order to gain more experience with a larger number of schools and during the autumn term of 1986 a further six secondary and sixteen primary schools joined the scheme. But signs were already becoming apparent that both the DES and, the emerging power on the educational scene, the Manpower Services Commission were actively encouraging an approach to INSET management and funding which had much in common with the evolving SFSD scheme in East Sussex. A series of DES Circulars (starting with 3/83 and culminating with 6/86 and a further draft circular dated April 87) and the MSC's, TRIST (TVEI-related in-service training) scheme added both support and urgency to these new developments.

In effect, the TRIST scheme funded and administered by the MSC was a precursor of things to come. To obtain money for in-service programmes related to pre-vocational education (in practice, loosely interpreted and allowing many activities extending beyond this) schools and colleges were required to identify their own INSET needs and ways of meeting them. Many LEAs and schools which took part began the process of building staff development policies as a result. The National Foundation for Educational Research (NFER) in England and Wales, through its Education Management Information Exchange (EMIE) programme, surveyed LEA responses to the new INSET arrangements. Baker (1986), who prepared the EMIE report, notes the considerable influence of the TRIST experience on planning for the new system. Because of participation in TRIST, most LEAs had already appointed staff development coordinators in the 'TRIST' schools and had required them to analyze their needs and prepare INSET plans. He concludes:

> The examination of questionnaire responses and papers submitted by LEAs shows that the TRIST scheme has been a powerful influence upon INSET development nationally. Several features of this influence can be identified:

(i)   increased recognition of the need to link INSET to specific change initiatives and to curriculum development:

(ii)   an increased volume of INSET, with many fresh ideas and considerable experimentation with more flexible funding;

(iii)   further stimulus to the development of school-focussed and school-based INSET;

(iv)   stimulus to the creation of more systematic support structures for INSET at both LEA and institution levels. (p. 17)

Circular 6/86 (DES, 1986) set the seal on this approach for all LEAs by requiring that proposals for the annual In-service Training Grant should be based upon policies.

> The Secretary of State will wish to assure himself that these proposals are related to systematically assessed needs and priorities, are set within balanced and coherent overall policies and plans and build appropriately on the strengths of current arrangements. (p. 7)

The Circular further expects that such planning arrangements 'ensure that appropriate account is taken of the expressed needs and views of teachers, schools and colleges...'. A further, draft, circular sent to all authorities in April 1987 (Local Education Authority Training Grants Scheme: Financial Year 1988–89) re-emphasizes and elaborates upon these requirements. The Secretary of State reminds authorities that their proposals should be based upon:

(a)   consideration of the training needs of all groups eligible under the scheme and of local needs and circumstances;

(b)   regular consultation with the individual teachers, lecturers and other potential trainees, with each school, college or other institution and with other interested bodies such as governors of aided schools and the appropriate diocesan authorities. (p. 2)

The main problem for all authorities is how to comply with these directions and particularly how to build into their INSET plans the needs of the schools and the teachers. LEAs have adopted many different approaches details of which are beginning to emerge (Baker,

1986). It is clear that some have begun the process by concentrating upon INSET coordinating structures involving LEA committees and advisory teams, others have sought to devise and offer to schools an overall programme of courses and activities from which to choose whilst others have required that their schools prepare staff development plans on the basis of detailed guidelines. Some have attempted to combine all three. But whatever the starting point and wherever the emphasis is put initially it is important that at some stage the various parts of the overall plan should come together to form a coherent whole. National priorities, LEA requirements, the needs of the schools and the needs of the teachers should all be represented in the annual programme for in-service training submitted to the DES for approval. At present there are considerable differences between LEAs in the degree of time and energy expended in ascertaining these different sets of needs and priorities and the emphasis given to any one in the overall plan.

The approach adopted by East Sussex forms much of the content of this book. Because it was already engaged in SFSD when TRIST and its successor GRIST (Grant-related in-service training, as required by Circular 6/86) entered the scene it tended naturally towards, what might be described as, a 'bottom up' approach to planning. In other words the nature of the overall INSET plan would be strongly influenced by the schools and the policies which they had produced through discussions with staff. Schools would undertake some of their own staff development work but information about what other forms of INSET might be required would be provided by the schools and would be analyzed and formed into a County plan through structures that would be devised especially to meet this problem. This 'bottom up' approach does not and should not preclude national or County priorities. These would be fed into the debate by officers through the forums created for the purpose. But the essence of the approach would remain — the schools and the teachers would have a major say in how the plan would be formulated and what it would contain.

To summarize, the SFSD project which began in April 1985 followed the initiatives of previous work, particularly the SITE project and the Schools Council School-Based Staff Development Project. It accepted the notion that INSET should combine internal and external expertise and resources and that schools should be responsible for identifying their own needs and planning their own programmes. It took staff development to mean both the development of the individual and the school, or sub-units within it. It concentrated upon the preparation and implementation of policies for staff development at school and county level and the coordination of school policies within an overall LEA plan.

It is worth repeating and expanding some of the points made in the preface about the nature and purpose of this book. It is based upon the experience of a project team, the members of which worked closely with a number of schools in preparing, implementing and evaluating school-focussed staff development policies. The lessons learned from this are important and will be of use to others who wish to follow a similar path. The various chapters offer advice and guidelines on establishing staff development needs within schools, negotiating and drawing up policies, the content of policies (with examples) and the place of appraisal within SFSD. Finally the way in which East Sussex is attempting to coordinate school and county policy is discussed within the broader context of GRIST. It is not intended to suggest to those in other LEAs that this is how it should be done. Rather, the message is that if an SFSD route is followed and schools are encouraged to prepare and implement their own policies then certain problems will arise. The book attempts to define these problems and suggest ways in which they might be overcome.

2 SFSD in Action

In April 1985 the seven pilot schools began the task of preparing a policy for school-focussed staff development. The main purposes of the exercise were to find out what was involved in producing such policies, what advantages there would be in so doing and what implications there would be for county INSET plans.

The entire team took part in the ongoing evaluation. From the beginning, as teacher fellows returned from their schools and discussed progress and problems with other project members, detailed notes were taken of issues which might later be important in assessing the outcomes. Teacher fellows also provided regular written reports and documents which they had used with their own staff and these were filed for future use. They were also asked to complete a self-evaluation report for their school in April 1986.

Each school was visited on at least ten occasions by either one of the directors, the coordinator or the evaluator of the project. During the visits, the teacher fellow at the school, the head and other members of staff were interviewed. Attempts were made to talk to those directly involved in drawing up and implementing the policy, those taking part in staff development activities and, importantly, those not involved or otherwise hostile to the idea. In all schools between 30 and 50 per cent of the teaching staff were interviewed.

By the end of the first year it was decided to extend the project in order to gain more experience with a larger number of schools and, during the autumn term of 1986, a further twenty-two schools joined the scheme. By this time, the ideas embodied in SFSD had become sufficiently widely known and accepted in the county for there to be many more volunteers to join the scheme than could be included. Representatives from each of these (mainly heads and deputies) were given three days introduction to SFSD and were required, in the remainder of the term, to draw up their policies. The progress reports from each of these schools and their actual policies provided a further important source of information. From an analysis of the data there emerged four important questions.

(i) *Feasibility*
How feasible is it to expect schools to draw up staff development policies which require them to identify and order their staff development needs?

(ii) *Activities*
What kind of activities are likely to be included in staff development programmes as a result of the analysis of needs?

(iii) *Integration*
To what extent might SFSD become an integral part of school life and what problems might hinder progress?

(iv) *Implications for dissemination*
Should all schools in the County produce a policy and, if so, what training and support would be needed for schools entering the scheme? How would this affect INSET policy in East Sussex?

These question are now considered in turn. It should be emphasized that the project was concerned with feasibility and procedures for introducing policies for SFSD and the evaluation concentrates upon this.

Feasibility

The pilot scheme proved to be an important learning experience for all concerned. It was soon realized that the terms used — 'school-focussed', 'staff development' and 'policy' were not readily understood. The range of views within the team was considerable. Some had actually joined the project under the assumption that it was about 'appraisal' and it took some time to dispel this idea and to distinguish between the two concepts.

Much of the team's time in the early stages was taken up considering what had been done elsewhere in terms of school-based staff development and in analyzing staff development needs. There was some useful literature on these themes and, in addition, various researchers and practitioners were invited to talk about their work.

Throughout the summer term the teacher fellows spent about three days a week in their own schools, planning and undertaking an analysis of staff development needs. They went about the task in a number of different ways. In one secondary school, particularly badly affected by industrial action, the teacher fellow wrote to all staff offering them an opportunity to discuss their needs from an 'individual, departmental and pastoral' point of view. Most responded and it seems that these interviews not only made staff think about their roles and their needs but also brought out feelings of discontent and frustration.

Another secondary school held a full staff meeting in school time to discuss SFSD. From this, there emerged a number of areas where it was felt the school should concentrate its efforts. This meeting was followed up by a number of informal discussions between the teacher fellow and interested members of staff. In both cases a draft policy document was prepared on the basis of the information gained.

The teacher fellow in the third secondary school arranged for SFSD to be discussed during several staff meetings held in school time and this produced some information concerning perception of needs. On the basis of this, but also using knowledge gained from career interviews with individuals (already part of the school's normal practice) the head drafted a policy document.

The primary schools adopted a mixture of approaches. Three used questionnaires distributed to all staff which were then analyzed by the teacher fellow. Two of these used an INSET day closure to discuss staff development and policy formulation and of these two, one head obtained further information by interviewing all members of staff about their staff development needs. The fourth primary school used a part of a day closure to discuss SFSD and this provided most of the information for the draft policy.

Whatever method was used to obtain information, it generally elicited sufficient data for the teacher fellow to prepare the first draft of a policy. This document, in its rough form, was then fed back to staff for further comment and discussion. But the extent of consultation which took place, before and after the policy statement was prepared, differed considerably between the schools and this had an effect on the subsequent commitment of staff to the whole idea of SFSD.

Decisions about the ordering of needs and the general control of the policy in operation also differed between schools. Policy documents normally contained statements regarding roles and responsibilities in the decision-making process and this became known as the policy 'structure'. In one primary school the head acted as the coordinator and decision maker but ensured regular consultation with staff. A similar situation existed in another primary school and in one of the secondary schools except that a deputy head filled the coordinating role.

In the remaining two secondary schools and one of the primary schools a staff development committee was created to which staff were elected to represent various interest groups. In the fourth primary school the staff as a whole were regarded as the decision-making body. Regular meetings after school were used to decide upon the form and operation of the policy.

The degree of staff involvement in important aspects of policy formulation and operation differed considerably, even in this small sample of schools, and largely reflected management style. The extent of participation had some interesting outcomes (not all of them predictable) in terms of staff commitment and scope of activities initiated. Nevertheless, it is possible to answer the first question concerning feasibility in the affirmative. It has proved possible, despite the difficult context, to draw up and implement policies in the pilot schools. Most schools actively sought ways of making time to engage in SFSD activities. It has also been shown that various structures can be created which enable decisions to be taken about priorities, direction and control.

Furthermore, the new schools entering the scheme in 1986 have shown that, by drawing upon the experience of the pilot schools, they have been able to prepare policies with considerably less training and discussion time than their forerunners.

Activities

The policies provided a means of combining and coordinating existing activities with new initiatives. To enable additional activities to take place each school was allocated a budget equivalent to the cost of one day's supply cover for each teacher in the school (with a minimum of £500 to compensate the small schools).

Visits to the schools revealed a wide range of activities which can be categorized as follows: in-school courses and workshops; specific programmes, small-scale investigations; mutual support; planned task experience; communications; reviews and appraisal; out of school activities such as visits and exchanges and external courses. These are now described in more detail.

School Organized Courses and Workshops

Four of the schools used INSET day closures to deal with various aspects of staff development. In some cases the day was devoted to identifying needs and agreeing upon action but in others the time was used for a workshop on a specific theme or problem such as classroom observation, timetabling and word-processing.

Otherwise, time has been found in two secondary schools in the evenings or weekends or through the judicious use of supply cover to arrange for staff-led seminars and workshops. The following topics were some of those covered: information technology, library skills, teaching methods in physics, classroom management, careers advice for pupils. These were mainly restricted to the secondary schools.

It seems likely that more of these activities would have taken place had it not been for industrial action and several schools have prepared programmes which will be implemented when the dispute is eventually resolved.

Specific Programmes

Three secondary and two primary schools have devoted time and resources to planning and implementing schemes for student teachers and probationers. The programmes include a structured introduction enabling the newcomers to better understand the workings of the school and also to meet people socially. Throughout the programme they are observed, have a chance to observe others and to discuss matters of interest and concern.

In one of the secondary schools a course was also devised, in conjunction with a special school, for those with formal pastoral responsibility. It was concerned with the care and control of disruptive pupils and to issues relating to maladjustment. Ten members of staff attended a series of seminars in school time over two terms. Supply cover was used to release them from their other duties.

Small-Scale Investigations

This usually involves one or more members of staff in problem-solving investigations into specific areas of concern followed by reporting back to appropriate groups. Examples include a review of the pastoral curriculum, the organization and lay-out of the classroom and mathematics and English teaching.

Mutual Support

Mutual classroom observation has formed a major part of the staff development programme in several schools. In one secondary school, pairs of teachers arranged regular exchange visits to the others' classroom followed by feedback sessions. In one primary school a more elaborate scheme was devised in which two or three members of staff work together and, within a set of guidelines agreed by the school, decide how the observation should be conducted and upon what aspects of teaching it should focus. A report form is completed which normally specifies some action agreed by the participants based upon the observation and feedback. One member of staff reported how anxious he felt a first:

> But as the weeks went by I realised that I was receiving constructive advice as well as compliments on my work. By the sixth session I was asking the observer to comment on certain aspects of my teaching where I felt I could do with advice.

In another secondary school, mutual observation formed part of the evaluation of an integrated humanities course in which three members of staff worked closely together in planning and teaching a two-term module. A video camera was used to provide material for detailed anlaysis of the teaching style of each member of the group.

In one primary school, the classroom observation is carried out entirely by the head who visits every teacher several times each term. The visits are now regarded as common-place and non-threatening by staff. The head always takes part in the lesson and spends time discussing the outcomes immediately afterwards.

Another form of support relates to the spread of knowledge and information to appropriate groups of staff after individuals have returned from workshops, courses or visits. Several schools have recognized that this knowledge is all too often retained by only one or two people and they have stipulated that in future a report should be made available to all staff or a 'teach-in' arranged. It is normally the staff development coordinator or committee who decide what action should be taken and this is sometimes agreed in advance, before the individual leaves for the course or visit. There is little doubt that such feedback is proving useful in helping to spread INSET information and also to enable other staff to decide whether to attend such courses in the future.

Communication

All of the pilot schools agreed that communication is an important aspect of staff development and all have taken some steps to overcome problems stemming from lack of information. A detailed written policy document was made available to all staff, setting out the aims, structure and programme relating to the scheme. In addition, each school either prepared, or updated, a staff handbook containing important information about school aims, policies, committees, roles, rules, activities etc. Several schools also decided that a special staff development notice board was necessary in inform staff of INSET opportunities both within and outside of the school.

Four schools set up a staff development library containing copies of educational journals, DES and HMSO reports or other books or documents requested by staff and considered useful by the coordinator or committee.

Job Experience

Two secondary schools regarded the deliberate planning of new job experiences as an important part of their staff development programme: one school called it 'job sharing' or 'shadowing'. The schemes, which are well supported, are based on the notion that applications for promotion are more likely to succeed if the applicant has gained experience of the appropriate tasks beforehand. In some cases a particular task such as timetabling, examinations, organizing parents' evenings or committee work may be shared or shadowed in this way but in others a teacher may carry out the full role responsibilities of another member of staff.

Reviews and Appraisal

Without any pressure from the project team, most of the pilot schools moved towards planning or carrying out some form of review or appraisal[1] as part of their staff development policy.

The heads of the four primary schools regarded 'job descriptions' as a key element in the review process although they were used differently in the different schools. One head argued that for effective review of a person's work to take place both reviewer and teacher should be clear as to what responsibilities each holds. A detailed job description should, therefore, clarify the nature of the role, its attendant tasks and also the expectations associated with it. The notion of sharing responsibilities and making them public was accepted by staff in the school and preliminary interviews were devoted to agreeing these with all teachers. A second primary school is now following a similar procedure. In one school negotiations about job description preceded and underpinned a more formal review scheme. One member of staff commented:

> We have also had the opportunity to draw up our own job description and to use it as a basis for our review at the end of the year. My review lasted for two hours and twenty minutes and I have nothing but praise for it. I was able to speak frankly and discuss my work of the past year and my aims for the future. During the normal course of events, this is not always possible.

In two of the secondary schools, 'professional', or 'career' interviews have preceded more formal staff development reviews. In one of the schools these are carried out by the head; in the other by a deputy head. They are open to any member of staff and deal with career planning, job applications and interviews. Pre-interview and post-interview briefings are also provided. In both schools the scheme links in with the job experience programme referred to above.

Three of the primary and one of the secondary schools now have staff development review or appraisal schemes and the two secondary schools that do not are in the process of devising one. Interviews are either done by the head or a deputy head and all are voluntary. The emphasis tends to be on staff development and teachers are asked to prepare beforehand by completing a pro-forma. In two of the primary schools, all staff have now been interviewed and in the third, about half have been involved. In the secondary school, about a third of the teachers have been interviewed. In four cases the head was the first to be interviewed and this normally involved an outsider (adviser or other head) as well as staff within the school.

Outside Activities

Visits and exchanges

One primary school devoted much attention to visits and in one year every member of staff was released for at least one visit. Most visits were to other schools, to observe 'good practice' or to improve liaison with the local secondary school. Some were to educational exhibitions. The other three primary schools also arranged visits but on a lesser scale.

From the secondary schools groups of teachers visited other schools and industrial firms. One school arranged over thirty visits to schools to observe teaching in maths, health education, careers, drama, geography, modern languages, microelectronics and remedial education. The same school also provided time for visits to industrial and commercial firms for several staff. Another secondary school arranged for several members of the maths department to make visits to a nearby school.

External courses

Short courses were also included as part of the programme for some schools. These were generally courses and workshops provided by advisers or by the University of Sussex, Brighton Polytechnic or another outside agency. They lasted anything from a day to twenty days. Some were in the evenings or at weekends.

The secondary schools have generally continued to make use of externally-based provision. One school in particular encouraged staff to follow up courses of relevance to them and eventually the release time granted totalled over 100 days in a year. But for two schools, external courses, both long and short, have remained a difficult area as far as their own policies are concerned. The schools are presented with the sensitive issue of how release time should be allocated and controlled. This depends upon where decision making power resides — with one person, a management team or a more broadly based forum such as a staff development committee. The last possibility can pose a problem for a head who does not wish to relinquish responsibility in this respect and it *could* lead to conflict with an elected staff development committee.

Existing or New Activities?

It was stated earlier that the policies had the effect of bringing together existing and new activities into a coherent statement. The question might therefore be asked — to what extent has the advent of SFSD policies stimulated new activities? The answer to this is partly obscured by the fact that some 'new' activities are actually an extension of existing ones. What has happened in some schools is that the discussion of certain ongoing activities in order to decide whether they should be included in the policy has brought them to the notice of a wider audience. Mutual classroom observation is a case in point. In one school this moved from being limited to two or three people to almost half of the staff.

Despite this, some fairly reliable evidence is available from the forms which schools are required to complete in order to obtain SFSD funding. In these they are requested to separate out existing activities from those which have been introduced with the policies. It seems that for most schools more than half of the activities are new and three schools approach the two-thirds mark. On this evidence it seems that the process of drawing up policies does stimulate additional activity.

Integration

Two years after the pilot schools first introduced their policies an interesting and uneven spread of progress and problems across the schools can be detected. The evaluation reveals different levels of implementation and acceptance of SFSD and corresponding variations in the degree of satisfaction amongst staff. A line of progress can be identified. At one end, SFSD is no more than a peripheral idea and has only limited effect upon the school. At the other end it has become an integral part of school life. Schools have reached various points along this dimension but the position is far from static and further progress is anticipated. It is proposed here to consider what factors limit or assist integration and what is achieved as a result of progress towards it.

SFSD as a Peripheral Activity

All schools inevitably started at the peripheral end of the scale as the ideas and possibilities associated with SFSD were first explained to staff. Their enthusiasm and subsequent commitment depended upon how it was presented to them, what involvement they had in drawing up the policy and what benefits they saw in it for themselves and for the school. But other important factors were identified during the evaluation.

One major barrier was the industrial dispute. This has affected all schools but some more than others. In one school, for instance, where the policy looked promising and broadly based, effective implementation depended upon the functioning of a staff development committee which could not meet. As a result, activities could only take place through initiatives on the part of the teacher fellow and, as the support of the committee was not forthcoming, most of the plans had to remain in abeyance.

Another factor which influenced the extent of SFSD acceptance and integration was the support and involvement of the head. In one school he remained cautious about the rapid implementation of SFSD and expressed concern about its effects upon the school and its pupils. The anxiety stemmed from the increasing amount of release time necessary to meet the growing demands of INSET courses of all types (not just those that have emanated from SFSD); a concern expressed by other schools in the past two years. He also expressed misgivings about the uncertainty surrounding INSET policy at national and County level and feared that the best laid plans of the school might be disrupted by courses advocated by the advisory service and others for which only short notice would be given. Mainly for these reasons he reserved his wholehearted support and this may have had a demotivating effect upon those teachers who would otherwise have supported the idea of SFSD.

Another factor which may have affected integration was the degree to which the policy and its implementation remained the responsibility of only one person. Although such an arrangement may succeed at first due to enthusiasm and commitment there is always the danger of the scheme collapsing if the person concerned has to withdraw for any reason. In one school the teacher fellow received the full backing of the head and was encouraged to take the main initiative in all activities, including calling and leading meetings of the newly-formed staff development committee. The problems arose when illness kept the teacher fellow away from the school for long spells. There was nobody else who could, or would, carry out the task. There are signs that the situation is now improving and that the head is beginning to take a more active role but SFSD must still be described as fairly peripheral.

What lessons can be learned from the schools that have not progressed far along the peripheral/integration dimension? On an optimistic note, it seems that the act of drawing up a policy is beneficial. It requires the analysis of needs and the thinking through and ordering of priorities. It means that, at least, some members of staff are involved in thinking about personal and professional development and the school's preparedness for change. Even limited action following the preparation of a policy may help some staff, and the potential for further progress, as outlined in the policies, always remains if the climate changes.

But the situations that have arisen in some schools also demonstrates the need for certain important conditions to be satisfied in the creation and continuance of SFSD. The first is the full and active support of the head and the second is the involvement of the majority of staff in the planning and implementation of the scheme. The need to share responsibility for leading the programme is clearly important to avoid loss of impetus if the coordinator leaves or is away for any length of time. These conditions will not guarantee success but they will provide a more solid base upon which to work.

Towards Greater Integration of SFSD

There are five schools which are now moving towards a greater acceptance of SFSD as an important aspect of school life, although some have moved further than others. One school in which SFSD has remained peripheral for some time has gradually used its management structure and style to expand the meaning of SFSD to meet its own ends. The school has a particularly active headteacher who believes that much of a head's time should be spent talking to staff or working in the classroom with them.

> When I visit the classroom, I'm an extra pair of hands. I believe in giving praise and encouragement which is what we all thrive on. Of course people have got weaknesses but bolstering their confidence can only help them overcome these.

Every teacher is observed several times each term by the head who has regular talks with them about their job description, teaching, other responsibilities and careers. Communication within the school is regarded by most staff as very good and a high level of solidarity and support for the school and its policies was noted, with very little dissension. The introduction of an SFSD policy has done several things. It has provided a new coordinating role for the deputy head, required the school to think through its priorities and order them more effectively and raised awareness about the need for staff development and the possibilities open to staff, individually and as a whole. The head enjoys teaching and getting to know pupils well and is always prepared to take classes thus freeing other members of staff for staff development activities. This is a school that should progress further towards a more integrated programme in the future.

Another school, because of the enthusiasm of the teacher fellow and its past record in terms of staff development, has made some progress but has faced severe limitations on action due to the ongoing dispute over pay and conditions. The teacher fellow, however, was determined to push forward with plans and to act whenever possible, despite the fact that the elected staff development committee could not meet. The result was that a wide range of activities involving several members of staff took place but not with the full support of the committee as would have been preferred. More recently the committee has met and some of the outstanding issues are now being dealt with. Also, an in-service day was recently used to establish priorities and to agree upon aims and objectives for the next stage of development. Again it is expected that the school will progress rapidly if the general educational climate improves.

In three schools SFSD might be described as almost a core element in the life of the school. Two of the schools, despite having heads with different management styles have involved all staff to a considerable degree in the planning and implementation of the schemes. In both cases there have been several full staff meetings to discuss the issue of SFSD followed by individual or small group discussions. In both schools the policy statements went through several drafts and staff were asked to comment at each stage. One of the schools also used a regular newsletter to keep staff up to date on progress.

In one school the teacher fellow saw it as a management responsibility to initiate and oversee SFSD. His role, he maintained, was to consult and inform extensively. There is little doubt that his energy and skill in this respect produced a committed group of staff. They agreed to start with an analysis and updating of job descriptions. Several teachers, when interviewed, suggested that the process of thinking through their job in this way, followed by discussion with the head, enabled them to realize their contribution to the school and far from being a daunting experience, it helped to boost their confidence. One commented: 'I began to realize how much I contributed to the school and it has made me feel more confident in applying for promotion'. It has led naturally to a range of staff development activities and to a feeling of team work and fulfilment amongst staff generally.

Another school has also moved towards a range of activities and to formal staff development review. Consultations were extensive but instead of the head acting as coordinator much of the responsibility was delegated to the staff through a whole staff committee. Those interviewed admitted that all activities, (many of them introduced on a trial and error basis) had been fully explained and had the approval of all staff. The well supported scheme for mutual classroom observation seemed to have created an 'open' climate and the impression gained was one of general enthusiasm for SFSD.

The final school appears something of an enigma having succeeded well with SFSD despite not having entirely fulfilled one of the conditions mentioned earlier. Here the range of activities engaged in has far exceeded any other school and the number of staff involved has been impressive. The head has been highly supportive and has clearly been keen to demonstrate how far the school has progressed in carrying out its programme. In a letter to the County Education Officer he states:

> Only four out of a teaching staff of seventy-four have not been involved; we have also involved a number of our supply and non-teaching staff... Overall the scheme has allowed us time for a systematic assessment of the needs of colleagues, and the results of those interviews have confirmed the productivity of this approach. We are now able to match more effectively need and provision; where a suitable course does not exist we have been able to produce an innovative response... The final result is we are getting much better value from INSET provision.
>
> The take up of the scheme has been particularly encouraging. At a time when morale is very low it has been responsible for improving practice within the classroom and producing positive responses by colleagues.

Where the scheme is unusual and might have been expected to have produced problems is in the nature and locus of the control of the programme. Staff were consulted in drawing up the policy but not to anything like the same extent as the two primary schools mentioned above. Many staff do not feel committed to the policy as such; for them it is a document produced by the management team. Implementation and coordination of the programme lie mainly with the teacher fellow (a deputy head) and it is largely due to unstinting efforts in selling the idea to individuals and departments and encouraging them to take part that the programme has proved so successful. Certainly this approach has paid off in a time of industrial problems and the fact that there have been few meetings has mattered little. The coordinator has generally been able to make decisions and move ahead and counters any criticism of this approach by remarking that if staff become involved and benefit from SFSD they will ultimately come to accept its aims and objectives.

In conclusion, therefore, it is reasonable to describe the outcome of SFSD in the seven schools as mixed but on the whole favourable. Having a policy will not by itself ensure that needs will be assessed, activities will be planned and staff will take part. Nor will SFSD instantly achieve major improvements in the quality of teaching, the working climate or the general organizational efficiency of the school. It is one approach to soundly based management in a time of rapid change. That it can offer something to schools and teachers has been demonstrated by the project so far and the results of the evaluation offer some guidelines for the next phase.

Implications for Dissemination

In the summer of 1986 a decision was made to extend SFSD to all schools in the county. All secondary schools will be required to produce a policy in the school year starting September 1987 and all primary schools will become involved over a two-year period beginning on the same date. This has implications for County policy and although the resources needed (including one-day supply cover per teacher for each school) have already been included or estimated for in INSET plans there are other implications which will have to be considered.

The second phase schools have been able to produce policies after a three-day training workshop attended by the head and one other member of staff. These policies are now available and for the most part they are of a reasonable standard and most show signs that they have been carefully thought through and discussed with staff. It must be remembered though that the time available to carry out this task was much less than that allowed for the original pilot schools and in order to complete the work by the deadline the schools have had to draw heavily upon the experience of their predecessors and the support of the project team. As the number of schools increases the support needed will also increase and this must be carefully planned. Unless there is help, encouragement and sensitive monitoring there will inevitably be the danger of skimping, especially given the other pressures that will face schools in the future.

What follows, therefore, is a set of issues suggested by the results of the evaluation which might usefully be studied by those in East Sussex responsible for overseeing the dissemination process. Attention to these points should help to anticipate some of the demands and problems that will inevitably arise.

(i)   Schools are responsible for producing policies to meet their *own* needs and it would, therefore, be wrong to impose a rigid set of rules as to what is expected. They should be encouraged to be autonomous and creative in their approach.

(ii)   However, experience has shown that schools do appreciate flexible guidelines and these can be provided without unduly restricting their autonomy. For instance, an outline of a policy document indicating the main sections normally included can be provided together with a costing form and an explanation as to what each school will be expected to pay for and what will fall within the separate, County INSET budget. The use of such a format will not affect the content of the policy and should help both the school and the county to draw together information more quickly and easily.

(iii)   Although there will be different management styles in the various schools, evidence from the evaluation indicates that there is a greater likelihood of achieving the aims of SFSD if staff are fully consulted and involved. It is recommended that in the training, support and monitoring process this principle be emphasized.

(iv)   If SFSD remains at the periphery of a school's activities it will have limited effect. But if it is adopted as a core aspect of policy and organization it can bring about considerable changes in attitudes and morale as well as activities. To achieve this it may be necessary to involve teachers in many of the key decisions concerning activities and priorities. Those managing schools should be both aware of and prepared for this.

(v)   Planning an SFSD programme means looking ahead for a least a year and ordering priorities within the limits of what is deemed advisable for each school. A desire to engage in many activities may have to be set against the possible disruption caused if too many staff are away for too long. Supply cover has its problems as well as its advantages. The outcome will often be a compromise, resulting in a finely balanced set of activities using a combination of in-school and after-school time. Several schools have expressed concern lest this fine balance be disturbed by other INSET requirements imposed upon them with only short notice. This suggests that a County INSET plan, in which essential activities for the forthcoming year are detailed, be made available to schools early enough for them to be considered as a possible part of their annual programme. This coordinating aspect of SFSD within the County plan may well be an essential condition for confidence in the scheme and its future success.

(vi)   Interviews with staff have proved to be an important adjunct to SFSD. In order to establish staff development needs for the school it is necessary to talk to teachers individually and the interview format provides a suitable opportunity for this to take place. Whatever the future may hold in the way of a central government imposed appraisal scheme it still seems reasonable, in connection with SFSD, to suggest that regular staff development interviews take place.

(vii)   Finally, with the inevitable emphasis on school needs as the basis for SFSD policies, the needs of the individual teacher should not be forgotten. Staff development is also concerned with career and professional development and in drawing up and implementing policies this is an important factor to bear in mind.

Summary

The evaluation of the project has revealed a number of important points about the preparation of an SFSD policy by each school. First, it has proved to be a feasible exercise and although some training is necessary this can normally be limited to two or three days for two members of staff (usually including the head). The drawing up and introduction of policies, in itself, stimulates new staff development activities. Provided staff participate in the process and the head is prepared to fully back the scheme there is, barring action associated with the industrial dispute, a good chance that SFSD will become an integral part of school life. The scheme as it is evolving is capable of forming an important part of the County's overall INSET plan and will do much to meet the demands of DES Circular 6/86 regarding consultation with schools and teachers in respect of staff development needs.

With these points in mind we now move on to a more detailed analysis of some of the issues raised by the project. Part 2 of the book will examine, the problem of needs analysis, methods of assessing needs and the place of appraisal or staff development review in the process.

Note

1 These terms are defined in chapter 5.

Part II
Assessing Staff Development Needs

In part 1, the reasons for creating an SFSD project were described together with its working philosophy, methods and outcomes. The evaluation of the scheme in the pilot schools revealed a number of possibilities and problems. The lessons learned from these will be used to extend the discussion to a number of key issues.

An important place to begin is with the identification and assessment of staff development needs. What kind of needs are there? Are schools and their staff aware of needs? How might they be formally assessed? Who should be involved? What is the place of appraisal or staff development review in the process? These are the main questions considered in part 2.

3   The Problem of Needs Assessment

Before beginning a detailed analysis of needs an important value position should be clarified. It concerns the main aim of staff development. Who is meant to benefit from the process? The fact that the major function of schools is the education of pupils is seldom denied, even if the type of education which should be provided is more problematic. Improvements in the organization of schools, the curriculum and the quality of teachers and teaching is, therefore, mainly for the benefit of the pupils. A common overriding aim often found in policy documents is:

> The purpose of staff development is to enhance the quality of pupils' learning.

This seems reasonable and the sentiment provides the central principle for what follows. But there are good reasons why it should share its position of pre-eminence with another principle which stems from the view that the effectiveness of organizations depends upon the quality of life provided for those who work within them.

Organizations exist for their employees as well as for their clients. This view stems from the work of researchers and theorists such as Argyris and Schon (1976), Sarason (1982) and Goodlad (1983) who offer a 'humanistic' approach to organization development. The broad argument is that the workplace is an important, often major, part of a person's life. It should, therefore, be designed to provide a humane and satisfying environment. Goodlad makes the point:

> Surely, too, if we can accept the concept of quality in industrial working life as good in itself, we can accept, equally, the goodness of quality of life in schools...
> It is high time, then, that we paid attention to the quality

of the school workplace, the conditions and practices that make it unhealthy, and how to create and maintain the healthiest ecosystem possible. (pp. 47 and 48)

In this chapter and the next, therefore, school-focussed staff development will be regarded as having two primary aims. The first is to benefit the pupils who attend school in order to learn and the second is to benefit those whose responsibility it is to facilitate that learning. It is assumed, also, that the two are connected; a more satisfying work environment for the teachers should ultimately benefit the pupils. The discussion which follows takes this to be the case.

With the above principle in mind, it seems reasonable to suggest that a carefully thought out school-focussed staff development policy will be based upon a thorough assessment of the needs of a school and its teachers. How else can the programme represent, and seek to achieve, the developmental goals of those involved? But how many schools and teachers can really demonstrate that they regularly collect evidence concerning their work and from this evaluate and, if necessary, modify their goals and attempt to improve their performance? Despite much talk about self-evaluation, the truth is that formal reviews are not generally regarded as an essential part of school life. And yet the importance of adequate needs assessment before embarking upon staff development exercises can hardly be overemphasized. Eraut (1987) makes a strong plea.

Looked at more globally, the profession as a whole and its capacity to improve the service is dependent on the quality of its needs assessment. Hence to enhance teachers' and administrators' capacities for making a good needs assessment must surely be a principal aim of staff development programmes. Needs assessment is not just a beginning, a first stage in formulating some new development or plan. It is also an end, essential to the profession's capacity to properly direct its resources and efforts to the ultimate benefit of our pupil clients. Needs assessment is not just a matter for consultation and report, it lies at the heart of the educational process itself. (p. 30)

The new DES funding arrangements for INSET described in part 1 make it clear that schools will be involved in reviewing their own staff development needs on a regular basis. The SFSD project has shown just how difficult an exercise this can be. The pilot schools had to learn as they went along. In this chapter and the next, the experiences of those schools and the problems they encountered are used to build a more comprehensive picture of what might be done to improve the process of needs assessment.

Awareness of Needs

Unless specific attempts are made to identify staff development needs, how might individuals, groups or organizations become aware of them? It seems that they are aware to some extent, for INSET provision has been based upon satisfying such needs for many years. Schools have organized INSET days, teachers' centres have provided various staff development activities, advisers or inspectors have offered LEA courses and colleges, polytechnics and universities have offered a wide range of long and short programmes: all of these, ostensibly, to meet staff development needs.

What happens in schools then may be fairly haphazard but it nevertheless generates sufficient awareness of need for some action to take place. This general awareness may not be at a very high level of sensitivity or urgency and it may not be clearly analyzed nor communicated from one person to another. For most people it may be no more than a sense of unease or a vague perception of dissatisfaction. There may be a feeling that all is not well, that things could be better or that problems may be building up for the future. Perhaps a solution may suggest itself, perhaps not. Where a way forward is sought a rapid decision may be made without thinking the problem through or considering the range of possible alternatives. Action may be taken with little or no consultation with others.

There may be indicators which signify the need for action. It is generally supposed that teachers have some idea of how well or badly things are going over a period of time. In the classroom, a person experiencing discipline problems might be aware of it as a result of the unintended activity which is taking place. The extent to which children are learning might also come through in the longer term: tests and examinations, for instance, generally provide some quantitative assessment on this score, however misleading this may be at times. Teachers may, consciously or unconsciously, inodify their ideas and attitudes on the basis of such feedback.

At the group or school level, other indicators may also be available. The attendance registers for children and the absenteeism rates for staff could be important pointers to organizational health. The extent to which formal disciplinary action is required to sanction pupil behaviour is a further possible indicator. And throughout the organization the level of morale might be gauged in numerous small ways such as the extent of extra curricular activity, the amount of parental involvement, general tidiness and the quantity and quality of displays of work indicating the level of pride taken by staff and pupils in the appearance of the school.

Teachers may also pick up clues as to the quality of their performance from others. In the classroom, enthusiasm and morale should be recognizable. And throughout the school day, and afterwards, the teacher is in contact with many people all of whom are possible sources of feedback. Most important in this respect are fellow professionals who share the teaching and the organization of the school. Meetings with such colleagues will take place informally and formally. The word in the corridor or the longer exchanges in the staffroom are potential sources of feedback on one's own work and the more general aspects of departmental or school performance. The conversations may not be directed towards staff development but they may contain concerns related to what seems to be lacking in specific situations. Problems on a school trip, noise in the library, lack of certain teaching materials, misinformation about the outcome of a meeting or complaints about its irrelevance, computers out of action again, concern about the way in which resources are allocated between different groups, a timetabling or room problem that crops up every term. These are all aspects of the functioning of an organization that could indicate staff development needs.

Staff meetings may also bring to the surface other areas of concern. These may be purposely placed upon the agenda or they may arise out of discussion concerning a particular issue. School or departmental meetings called to discuss curriculum initiatives generated from outside of the school, for instance, may raise the matter of staff development. 'But who have we got who can do the job — plan, coordinate, teach etc?' is a question which may be raised at such meetings. Or a concern voiced by one person that the new maths scheme does not seem to working too well may provide another stimulus for debate regarding the need for more coordination or more training. The head or management team could be noting and acting upon these matters but the general discussion may also be affecting the awareness of each member of staff present. Other forms of feedback may be provided through informal meetings with parents, governors or advisers, or teachers from other schools or LEAs. Remarks made may often be chance or unintended but they may have an effect if the teacher is in a receptive frame of mind.

So there is much going on in most schools that *could* lead to the identification of staff development needs. But will it? How much are teachers and heads sensitive to the indicators mentioned and even if they are how and in what ways will they translate their perceptions into action? Is there not a danger that 'needs blindness' stemming from complacency, tradition, and possibly out of date and incorrect assumptions about what is actually happening in the classroom may result in no action at all. Or if action does take place might it not be random, haphazard and unequally distributed across the school as a whole? In many schools this is probably the situation and will remain so unless some deliberate steps are taken to improve matters.

Variety of Needs: An Example

The complexity of needs in most organizations is considerable. Imagine, for a moment, the view of a school that might be gained by a relatively, neutral observer; someone who knows the school and its staff very well but is able to step outside and view it fairly objectively without too close an involvement in its day to day activities. Perhaps a senior teacher on secondment might be able to do this or a recently retired head or an adviser who has developed a close relationship with a school over a long period. What might they see that could give rise to staff development needs as they look in at the school? Here are some examples from a hypothetical school that clearly has some problems.

The general climate seems to lack something. There is no sense of purpose. Management, whilst fair and humane, lacks bite and initiative. Ideas from the teaching staff are seemingly encouraged but they usually founder in endless meetings or from lack of support or resources. Communications seem to be poor and there is often conflict because people are unaware of exactly what is expected of them and what they might reasonably expect of others. Participative management is encouraged through policy statements but nobody seems very clear what this means in practice nor how the several committees set up since the idea was mooted some years ago have actually improved things. The head is generous in always supporting requests from staff to attend INSET courses but this often places a heavy burden on those who stand in for them or else it involves more supply cover which some consider disruptive for the pupils. Few people have any idea how the courses attended have benefited either the individual concerned or the school and its pupils.

Next, the observer might note that there has been a change over the years in the intake of pupils. There are now many more ethnic groups represented and since 1981 there are also more children classified as having special needs. The school is in a falling rolls situation but appears to be affected more by this than its neighbours. There has been an increase in absenteeism and there have been hints of a drugs problem. There is, though, a general shortage of information amongst staff on many of these issues and a marked lack of discussion on most.

The outsider might also have noted that a certain subject department has a policy for the curriculum but that there have been few meetings to discuss this. Most teachers are only vaguely aware that such a policy exists and have very little idea as to how it affects them in their day to day teaching. Also it might have been noted that pastoral care has been much discussed but has remained an issue that most people are still uncertain about both in the way that it should be dealt with and their particular responsibilities towards it.

Finally, the outsider might also recall individual teachers. There are a few that are remembered because they are regarded by their colleagues as weaker members of the teaching establishment; they have the habit of upsetting people, they cannot be relied upon, they have not kept themselves up to date in their subject, they are limited in the range of teaching approaches they can call upon, they are poor in establishing a good rapport with their pupils, they take very little part in the life of the school outside of the classroom and they seem to have become cynical and demotivated. But the majority are not like this. Most are remembered as dedicated and efficient teachers but some have become frustrated with the school and feel under-valued. Some are happy enough but need more variation in the work they do, others seem uncertain as to where they should go next and require sound advice as to their career prospects and what might enhance their chances of promotion.

This pen picture is entirely hypothetical and is intended simply to bring together a number of problems which illustrate the variety of sources from which staff development needs might be identified. Embedded within this example are needs associated with the pupils, the curriculum, the teachers and their departments and the school and its management as a whole. These categories are considered next.

Categories of Need

The hypothetical example set out above illustrates both the variety and complexity of need for staff development within an organization.

In order to begin a needs analysis it is necessary to decide which aspects of an organization will come under scrutiny. The SFSD project team found that there were four essential aspects to be considered: the client, the curriculum, the individual member of staff (including the head and all teachers irrespective of the amount of teaching they do) and the organization (including sub-units such as departments and year groups).

The Client

For the purpose of this discussion the client is taken to be the pupil. There are many groups which may be regarded as indirect clients, all of whom may compete in some way to influence the kind of education provided. These include parents, community, religious bodies, employers, government etc. In a sense they are clients but they stand behind and help to determine the needs of the pupil.

The pupil as a focus for, and ultimately the beneficiary of, staff development will be affected when, for instance, a teacher sees the need to become more sensitive to individual learning needs or to improve the keeping of records, or the school seeks to prepare a policy for welfare or for careers advice. In other words the needs of the pupils are first analyzed in order to determine what kind of staff development is required.

The Curriculum

The curriculum may also provide the focus of attention. Curriculum development often leads to, or demands, staff development. New styles of teaching associated with say the introduction of a new reading scheme into a primary school or a pre-vocational programme into a secondary school or further education college, new forms of assessment, attempts to provide greater integration of subjects, student-centred learning, modularization etc. may all require staff development of some kind. The introduction of GCSE illustrates how much staff development is needed in certain cases. It may also have become apparent to many schools and departments just how inadequate the analysis of needs has actually been in this respect.

The Individual

The focus here is upon the individual member of staff. In what areas should that person seek, or be encourged to seek, further development? This may be motivated by the desire for career advancement, greater job satisfaction, improved performance or any aspect of personal development. Through self-analysis, discussions with colleagues or an appraisal interview, a teacher (including those in management positions) may decide that certain steps are necessary to improve their teaching or their professional development. This may be achieved by, for instance, gaining new experience, acquiring new skills, improving knowledge, gaining better qualifications or seeking greater self-knowledge.

Staff development might, and some would argue should, include all staff within the school. Thus, clerical and other support staff might also form the focus for the analysis of needs. Although some schools within the SFSD project included secretarial staff within school-based staff development activities (for instance secretaries were invited to workshops on using the computer and on pastoral care) the extension of staff development policies to include all ancilliary staff has generally not taken place. It may well be that there are sufficient problems to be dealt with in drawing up effective policies for teaching staff at present and that a wider definition of 'staff' to include others who form an essential part of school life must take its turn.

The Organization

Finally, the organization may be the focus for staff development in two senses. The first is related to improved organizational functioning through administration and management involving, for instance, better communication, more effective use of resources, enhanced morale and so forth. These effects will probably benefit clients and staff also but the focus of the development is primarily upon the functioning of the organization or its sub-units. In another sense, however, because the organization is the school, it embraces all of the above mentioned needs and depends for its effective working upon achieving an optimum balance between the needs of the client, curriculum, individual teacher, functional groups and administration/management.

It may sometimes be necessary for those in a school to focus upon several categories in relation to a particular problem or change. Take for example the area of special needs. Since the 1981 Education

Act, LEAs have responded in different ways but, in general, schools have been required to extend their provision for children with special needs. The immediate focus here is upon the client but this has all kinds of implications: for the school as a whole; for remedial, counselling and other welfare support units within it; for academic departments and their curriculum and for individual teachers and their teaching approach and general attitude to children with special needs. A problem area such as this indicates the necessity for staff development in all four categories referred to earlier.

Other examples of broadly-based issues which have implications for analysis in more than one category include: staff development needs raised by demographic change in the community resulting in a multicultural intake to a school; the introduction of pre-vocational education; the wider use of computers throughout the school or the introduction of an appraisal scheme. The list could be extended depending upon the type of school or college and its particular circumstances. The point is made, however, that the school should be aware of a host of possible needs for staff development which could be analyzed according to the four categories. Some examples of the ways in which this might be done are dealt with in the next chapter.

Summary

The analysis of needs should both precede the drawing up of a staff development policy and form a continuing part of policy implementation and revision. Generally, there is some awareness of needs arising out of the day-to-day activities of a school but there is seldom a formal analysis nor a clear ordering of priorities. Needs are generated by a complex set of factors but these can be categorized as those relating to: the client, the curriculum, the individual member of staff and the organization as a whole.

4   Assessing Needs: Methods and
       Perspectives

It most schools the identification of staff development needs tends to be haphazard and is often left to chance. In this chapter the possibilities for a more formal, extensive and coordinated approach are considered. A number of methods are reviewed first and then the problem of perspective — who should assess needs? — is discussed.

Methods

In recent years various ideas and schemes have been tried as a means of, directly or indirectly, identifying staff development needs. The categories of need suggested in the last chapter — client, curriculum, individual and organization — provide a useful set of headings under which to consider such methods and these will be used again in this chapter.

Some points of clarification are, however, necessary. The distinction between the assessment of needs and staff development itself is not always clear and in practice there is often an overlap. Some activities classified as staff development lead on naturally to the identification of needs whereas some exercises, intended primarily to ascertain needs, are in themselves a form of staff development. In the former category might fall mutual classroom observation or shadowing a pupil for a day. These will quite probably suggest needs for staff development. In the latter category, a workshop used by a school or department to identify its INSET needs may possibly result in other group problems being dealt with at the same time. For present purposes the distinction is not important and if assessment of needs merges into staff development or vice versa this can only serve to make the process more effective.

It should also be noted that some exercises which are primarily intended to serve purposes other than the assessment of needs may in practice contribute to this process. A whole school review, for instance, may lead to a restatement of school aims, to curriculum developments or to changes in organization. From these, however, there will usually emerge the need for staff development of some kind.

The Client

The pupil, as a source of information for staff development needs, is a relatively recent focus of attention. Certainly, teaching and learning outcomes in the form of test and examination results have always provided some feed-back but interest has shifted to the process of learning and the pupil's thoughts, feelings and problems. It is argued that a great deal can be gleaned about one's teaching if serious attention is paid to the opinions of those on the receiving end. But how is such information obtained?

An Open University course (Open University, 1981) aims to equip teachers with the skills necessary to evaluate aspects of their practice, particularly in relation to what pupils actually do and what they learn as a result. Teachers are encouraged to seek the views of pupils in evaluating their work. Baker (1984) has edited a series of case studies in a Schools' Council booklet *Practical Self-Evaluation for Teachers*. Many of these add a further dimension to the possibilities of obtaining evidence from pupils and using it for staff development purposes. The methods include, observation, discussion, interviews, questionnaires, pupil diaries, audio and video tape recordings etc. The booklet contains several examples of simple questionnaires that were used effectively with pupils. Comments from those involved illustrate the staff development outcomes.

> The project has also influenced my teaching style. I try to listen to more children talking more of the time. I am much more relaxed in my approach to teaching. The tasks I set tend to be more discussion-based, working with either pairs or larger groups. (p. 21)

> As a result of my work this year I have modified my question and answer sessions so that I do not dominate so much, I am more conscious of the length of introductions before practical

work and the time I spend with pupils. I am much more aware of aspects of my teaching than I used to be, largely because I have had to think about my teaching style and its imperfections. (p. 31)

An evaluation course for heads of science at the University of Sussex in 1986 set a pre-course task as follows.

Choose two pupils in your department of varying ability from the second or third year, whom you are not currently teaching.

For each pupil arrange to observe them for a double period (without their knowing that they are the focus of your attention). As soon afterwards as practicable have a brief discussion with them about their experience of the lesson. It may be necessary to remind them of various phases of the lesson, and useful to organise the discussion around what they have written in their books. Then try to discover what scientific concepts and ideas that formed the substance of the lesson's content mean to them. What is their understanding of them, and what do they see as their significance?

As the evaluation course progresses more pupils are studied using interviews and questionnaires and profiles are produced. One head of science who involved other members of his department, wrote about the outcomes of the exercise as follows.

...the following changes have taken place, as...a direct result of the profiles.

1 Drastic increase in practical work by all members of the science staff...
2 Effort made to make practical work more relevant...
3 Move away from didactic and book orientated teaching styles.
4 Increase in the number and variety of out of school activities.
5 Better staff/pupil relations.

Another approach used in the SFSD project involves shadowing a pupil for a day. The observer sits in the same lessons, takes the same breaks and discusses the experience with the pupil at the end of the day. This has sometimes had a profound effect on the observers causing them to re-think their own approach to lessons.

The Curriculum

Curriculum review and evaluation is a major topic in its own right and has its own body of specialized literature. It is not the intention here to examine the subject in any depth but rather to remind policy makers that review and evaluation may often lead to change and that such change may involve staff development of some kind. Curriculum review will often raise questions about aims and objectives, course content, teaching and learning methods, the provision of teaching and learning materials, assessment and more generally what Parlett and Hamilton (1981) call the 'learning milieu'.

The methods used to obtain information in all of these areas are numerous and the approaches are often determined by specific philosophical standpoints. Comprehensive overviews are provided by, for instance, Open University (1982), Shipman (1983) and McCormick and James (1983).

Reviews and evaluations may be carried out by individual teachers in their own classrooms, by others who teach on the course or by departmental teams specifically created to undertake the task. A range of approaches may be used including the analysis of course documents and learning materials, classroom observation, interviews with pupils and staff, tape recordings, questionnaires etc. This data, when analyzed, will produce a profile from which areas of concern will generally be derived and, from these, needs for staff development identified. For example if dissatisfaction with teaching methods is identified as a problem it may seem appropriate to organize for those involved to: visit other classrooms or other schools, be observed themselves over a period, attend a course on alternative teaching methods, form a team to work out a new teaching approach etc.

Alternatively, if the teaching materials are found to be unsatisfactory, individuals or groups may be encouraged to review other possible sources or to prepare or adapt materials themselves. This, in turn, may require attendance at a workshop or course on producing materials which might be organized within the school or possibly at a teachers' centre.

So far, the focus on the curriculum has been concerned with particular courses but this might be extended to cover a broader curriculum area such as pre-vocational education. An interesting example of this approach to the analysis of needs is provided by the Further Education Unit (FEU, 1982) in the report *Teaching Skills*. Here attention is focussed upon the needs of teaching staff in response to the introduction of courses for vocational preparation such as TVEI

(Technical, Vocational Education Initiative) and CPVE (Certificate of Pre-Vocational Education). A checklist of needs created by such courses was produced by the FEU following a survey of those involved in a number of schools and colleges. It was noted for instance that these courses generally required: curriculum innovation, a shift towards a more student-centred approach, new methods of teaching, team work and the ability to liaise and negotiate with staff and students. To what extent could staff cope with these new demands?

The report suggests that course teams construct a list of questions related to available experience for each of the above. Members of the team should then answer each question individually and through group discussion. The aim should be to produce a profile of the group's strengths and weaknesses in relation to the different demands made by the new curriculum. The report lists a typical set of questions which might arise:

> To what extent are staff confident...that they have had successful experience of student-centred curriculum:
>
>> by teaching within a flexible curriculum framework which seeks to integrate different subject and/or vocational studies;
>>
>> by negotiating with the learners an approach which seeks to work from their perceived and/or identified needs; and both recognizes and acts upon feedback from them;
>>
>> by supporting learners with counselling and guidance;
>>
>> by providing learners with formative as well as summative assessment in a systematic way, perhaps through the operation of checklists, student profiles and/or appraisals; and
>>
>> by providing relevant and appropriate learning experiences.

From the answers to these questions it should be possible to see in what areas the team, and the individuals within it, require opportunities for staff development, and the kind of activities which might be appropriate.

Thus, by focussing attention upon the client and the curriculum and obtaining and analyzing data, areas where staff development needs arise can be recognised. By changing the focus to the individual and the organization, additional needs may identified which will add further to the stock of information available.

The Individual

The third category focusses upon the individual teacher and will be concerned with both self-appraisal and evaluation by others. What is involved in the first instance is a deliberate attempt by an individual to evaluate various aspects of his or her own work. The process often involves personal introspection; delving into thoughts and feelings regarding goals, activities, successes and problems. It is, of course, entirely feasible to do this on a regular, informal basis and some teachers would suggest that, consciously or unconsciously, this is part of their normal working life. But it might also be argued that the process of self-analysis can be encouraged and helped by deliberately planned activities of some kind as suggested later. The second approach is through the involvement of others who may observe the teacher in action and or act as a sounding board for ideas and perceptions.

Some possibilities for self-evaluation and evaluation by others are now considered.

Self-evaluation questionnaires

Questionnaires are sometimes used to stimulate thinking about specific aspects of teaching. Attempts by a respondent to find a satisfactory answer to carefully designed questions may sometimes result in insights into areas that require attention or development. Various forms are available for different purposes. For instance, a general, but fairly adaptable set of questionnaires is produced for managers by Woodcock and Francis (1982) in association with their book *The Unblocked Manager*. The intention is, through guided reflection, to recognize 'blockages' which prevent effective and satisfying work and to identify steps necessary for overcoming the problem. A similar approach is used in relation to a scheme for *Management Self-Development* (Boydell and Pedler, 1981). The following is a typical set of questions from this scheme:

Sharing Experience

(a) How important to you is sharing experience with colleagues on common problems?

(b) How satisfied are you with opportunities to share experiences with colleagues on common problems?

Reasons for answers. (p. 237)

Respondents are required to tick — 'of great importance', 'of some importance', 'not important' or 'completely unimportant' against each question. The scheme also contains guidelines for interpretation and analysis. The questions above might, if used by a teacher cause them to reflect upon organizational and interpersonal aspects of their work.

But perhaps the greatest use of self-evaluation forms is (or is likely to be) in connection with appraisal schemes. Here it is becoming the practice to require a teacher to complete a questionnaire or pro-forma before an appraisal interview. The DES sponsored report *Those Having Torches* (Graham, 1985) and the ACAS report on appraisal/training (ACAS, 1986) both contain examples of forms used for this purpose. Some are very detailed and relate specifically to pre-defined areas of work such as lesson preparation, conduct of lessons, pastoral care etc., whilst others are shorter, more simple and open-ended. One form simply asks the teacher to define the key areas of the job under no more than six main headings and to answer the question in relation to each of them — 'How would you gauge your effectiveness in your defined job during the last year'.

The kind of questionnaire used in any situation will clearly depend upon its purpose and the general feeling of the staff towards its use. Pre-designed forms may be more suitable for some purposes, especially where time is at a premium or the exercise is seen as an experiment to try out the idea. For many purposes, though, much can be gained if those concerned help to design their own forms. The questions are then likely to be more appropriate and the sense of ownership greater.

Appraisal interviewing

Appraisal has a number of different purposes one of which is normally taken to be — the identification of staff development needs. If the interview is based upon mutual trust, if confidentiality is observed and if the discussion is supported by sound information about a teacher's work and the context in which it is carried out then an interview can be an extremely valuable part of needs assessment. Its value was recognized by the project team in relation to SFSD but it has proved to be a controversial issue in the context of the industrial dispute. For this reason it is treated separately and at some length in the next chapter.

Peer counselling

Peer counselling is based upon the idea that feedback from another, trusted person is an important part of self-analysis and development. Reflection is made more penetrating and effective as a result of probing using non-judgemental questions. A framework for this approach is set out by Elliott-Kemp and Rogers (1982). The underlying principle is this:

> A person-centred approach takes an optimistic stance towards people and growth; people are basically good, and capable of self-directed development. (It does not really make sense to talk of developing someone else — ultimately, the only valid development is self-development.)
>
> A person cannot, however, develop in a vacuum: we need each other. We need to augment our personal introspection with feedback about our behaviour from others. (p. 35)

This approach was used in an interesting way in a staff development day at a college and is described by Field and Mulhern (1983). They organized the day on the principle that:

> Genuine self-evaluation means looking at not only what you feel about yourself, but also at what other people feel about you, so it is important to seek the opinion of others — your peers, your students, your principal and vice principal — but the emphasis must be on seeking the views of others. You are asking for other people's views of you so that you can take them into consideration when you value yourself. (p. 599)

Individuals were first asked to list their strengths in their job. They were then asked to form pairs and to present to their partner the strongest case they could in support of a hypothetical application for their present post at the college. In groups of eight each person then made the positive case for their partner to the group. This was a confidence and trust building exercise.

Part 2 required individuals to write down their thoughts on their own development for the coming year. They were also asked to respond to a list of possibilities regarding various forms of development and to add to the list as they saw fit. Again the exercise was followed by a discussion in pairs as to how their needs compared with those of the other person and of possible ways of meeting such needs.

Mutual classroom observation

This might be considered a part of, or an extension to, the peer counselling described above. We are not concerned here with classroom observation as part of a formal appraisal scheme, although such might have been included, rather, with the provision of feedback on teaching skills by a trusted colleague. Tamsett (1982) describes a 'teacher-teacher partnership in the observation of classrooms'. The method is summarized as follows:

> An approach was developed in which pairs of teachers in the same school entered into partnership, alternating the roles of 'teacher' and 'observer', the teacher who was to act as observer being invited into the partner's classroom to comment on issues nominated by the partner as a source of concern in teaching. The partners met after the observation to discuss the observer's comments. The teachers agreed not to discuss their observations outside of the partnership. (p. 66)

There are numerous possible variations on this theme. In the SFSD project, for instance, in one school, three teachers were involved in visiting each others classrooms. There is also no necessity for the issues to be restricted to those nominated by the person teaching. In fact some would argue that as trust develops it is important to have a greater input of observer perspectives on problems and issues which may not be recognized by the teacher concerned. Perhaps the most important point, however, is that the ground-rules for observation and feedback should be negotiated and agreed by those concerned. The process should, ideally, lead to developmental steps being taken to improve teaching in those areas jointly agreed by those involved and consequently the activity might reasonably be considered staff development. The importance of classroom observation in the present context, however, is the contribution which it can make to the analysis of needs for individual development.

The Organization

Finally, staff development needs may be identified through a school self-evaluation exercise. There are now a considerable number of schools which do this as shown by the Open University's 'Review of school and college initiated self-evaluation activities in the United Kingdom' (James, 1982). Furthermore, in 1981, the Schools Council held a conference on school self-evaluation and the subsequent report

(Nuttall, 1985) provides examples of schemes in several local authorities. The conference led to a project from which emerged the GRIDS scheme — Guidelines for Review and Internal Development in Schools — (McMahon *et al*, 1984) setting out details for primary and secondary schools wishing to follow this approach.

The GRIDS scheme begins by making four important points. First, the aim is to achieve internal school development and not to produce a report for formal accountability purposes. Secondly, the main purpose is to move beyond review into development. Thirdly, the staff of the school should be involved in the process as much as possible and finally, decisions about what happens to reports should rest with those concerned in the review.

The scheme involves a survey of staff opinion regarding various aspect of school life including: the curriculum (for example, communication skills and creative work in the primary school or the lower school curriculum and careers education in the secondary school); pupils (for example, methods of grouping or pupil records); staff and organization (for example, roles and responsibilities or communication between staff) and links with people outside of the school (for example, parental involvement or relationships with school governors). The school is thus seen in its broad role as an organization which seeks to balance and coordinate several potentially competing sets of needs.

The questionnaire devised for the survey contains about forty specified items and room for teachers to add more if they so wish. Against each item staff are asked to indicate whether it would benefit from a specific review and whether the activity is currently regarded as strong, satisfactory or weak.

Thus, for example, in the primary school scheme the following items are included.

	Would benefit from specific review		
	Yes	*No*	*Don't Know*
Topic work			
Extra-curricular activities			
Pupil reports			
Consultation and decision-making procedures			
Parental involvement in the school			

Each member of staff is required to tick the appropriate box in relation to each item. The GRIDS process is divided into five stages. Stage 1 is called getting started and describes management's role and the process of consultation. Two is the initial review or survey and involves detailed planning, the distribution of information, the completion of the survey document and the analysis of the responses. This should indicate a number of priority areas which will form the basis for discussion amongst staff followed by stage three which requires one or more specific reviews to take place. For example, if, from the survey and discussion 'topic work' was generally regarded as weak and likely to benefit from a review, a team would be selected to undertake a detailed study. The team's report would later be made available to all staff and stage four then becomes action for development including meeting *'the in-service needs of the teachers involved in the development'*. Stage five is called 'overview and restart' and involves a reconsideration of the whole process, the introduction of improvements to the GRIDS procedures if necessary and restarting the cycle to focus upon other areas for specific review.

The booklets describing the process are clearly written and any school wishing to engage in GRIDS should have little difficulty in following the guidelines or adapting the scheme to meet its own particular circumstances. The examples given in the booklets indicate various needs which might be identified from using this approach and the different forms of action which might result. Staff development is prominent amongst them. Several schools in the SFSD project have used this approach. A number of LEAs have also produced their own guidelines to assist schools in the process of review and evaluation (for example, ILEA, 1977; Hampshire, 1984; Myers, 1987).

Other questionnaire surveys more directly related to staff development provide further possible means of establishing needs. They were also used by schools in the SFSD project and they provided a relatively quick way of obtaining information. Details of this approach are contained in another Schools Council report — *School-based Staff Development Activities* (Oldroyd, Smith and Lee, 1984). The example questionnaire asks the teacher to consider needs under three headings: as an individual, for the functional group and for the school as a whole. The questions and responses can easily be contained on two sheets of paper and it is suggested in the report that the forms be given to staff during a staff meeting or INSET day when the purpose and procedures can be fully explained and discussed.

One of the problems of using a questionnaire, however, is that it limits the likely responses because of the formulation of pre-set questions. More expansive and in-depth replies will normally be obtained through interviews when the person is encouraged to reflect upon his or her work.

Sub-groups

Most schools are sufficiently large for staff to belong to sub-groups formed for various purposes. The department is perhaps the most easily recognized, particularly in secondary schools and colleges, but groups are formed in most schools to carry out a number of different tasks associated with, for instance, pastoral work, curriculum development, reviews, special problems etc. It is within these groups that negotiations about the nature of the work and the expectations which people have of each other takes place. Elliott-Kemp (1986) notes the importance of such groups in relation to change. 'Indeed the hinge of change and development in the school is seen as the face to face staff group and the key process as interpersonal encounter'. These groups, whatever their function and upon whatever aspect of school life they choose to focus can, and should, be regarded as an important source of information regarding staff development needs.

Oldroyd, Smith and Lee (1984) provide an example of a review carried out by a group of humanities teachers from a secondary school during a day workshop at a local teachers' centre. After a brief introduction by the head of faculty the day was divided into three main sessions.

1   Retrospective. 'What I like least about our faculty.'
2   Introspective. 'What I am happy about in our faculty.'

Both sessions involved individuals writing out their views, followed by discussion in groups of three and then reporting back.

The afternoon session was called:

3   Prospective 'What we would like to achieve next year'.

This involved individuals writing down personal targets under three headings: classroom teaching, resource production and relationships, followed by a discussion and agreement of targets for the faculty. The report on this example of group activity notes that a strong sense of group ownership emerged and ensured that the targets were vigorously pursued.

Further examples of reviews at school or department level can be found in the Open University survey (James, 1982), the Schools Council Project on school self-evaluation (Nuttall, 1985) and *Becoming a Better Teacher* (Cumming *et al*, 1985).

Summary

The methods suggested above for the assessment of staff development needs can be summarized in tabular form. They are not all directly related to needs assessment but they will generally provide information in this connection.

Table 1 Summary of methods for establishing staff development needs

Category	Possible methods
Client	*Focus on Pupil* Interviews, Profiles Observation pupil for a day'
Curriculum	*Focus on curriculum* Interviews (pupils and staff) Questionnaires, Observation Analysis of materials Identify new demands on staff arising from new courses.
Individual	*Focus on teacher* Self-evaluation Appraisal interviews Classroom observation Peer counselling.
Organization	*Focus on school or sub-units,* Whole school review Departmental review

Perspectives

The various schemes, activities, questionnaires, interviews etc. outlined above, together, offer a number of opportunities for assessing need. They may raise general awareness of need; they may provide new or additional information, they may offer a new sense of direction and they may increase motivation to engage in staff development activities. Furthermore, as stated earlier, they are often, in themselves, a form of staff development.

But there are other issues associated with needs assessment and these stem from the problem of perspective. From whose viewpoint will needs be assessed? How will they be interpreted and what action will be taken as a result? It is possible that there might be more than one perspective in respect of each of the categories of need outlined above. Those which have proved to be influential in the experience of the SFSD project are — the teacher, the functional group and the school management. In addition there are perspectives outside of the school to consider and these include mainly the LEA and also Central government agencies such as the DES and MSC. The perspective from each standpoint is not always clear and straightforward and, in itself, may represent a compromise between competing interests. Nevertheless a dominant view can usually be detected and its influence discerned. If these perspectives are arrayed in relation to categories of need an overall picture, which illustrates the complexity of the matter, begins to emerge.

Table 2 Needs Assessment: Categories and Perspectives

		Category		
Perspective	Client	Curr'm	Indv.	Orgn.
Teacher →	1	2	3	4
Functional group →	5	6	7	8
School management →	9	10	11	12
LEA →	13	14	15	16
DES/MSC →	17	18	19	20

The matrix can be interpreted as follows. The teacher, any functional group within the school, the school management, the LEA or outside agencies such as the DES and the MSC may perceive the need for development in any of the categories (columns) which generate staff development needs — client, curriculum, individual member of staff or school organization. The perspectives may or may not coincide but, where there are differences, problems may arise.

For example, a teacher's view of her own staff development needs (box 3) may differ radically from the perception of her needs formed by her departmental colleagues and head of department (box 7) or by the school head or management team (box 11). Or, to take another example, the DES (box 18), the LEA (box 14) and the school (box 10) may all take different views on the amount and kind of staff development necessary in connection with proposed curriculum changes. The potential for competing views on the different categories is clearly considerable.

The problem is compounded by the possible difference between 'wants' and 'needs'. What people think they want may not necessarily be what they need. The same can apply to groups and to organizations. McGregor Burns (1978), writing about leadership, draws out the distinction between wants and needs. He suggests that effective leaders may often see beyond the immediate wants of their followers and work towards satisfying seemingly more important but, less recognized, needs. The implication is, that to understand needs, a vision is necessary of how things might be better for all concerned in the future. This requires a strategic, corporate and longer term view which may override the shorter term wants of individuals.

Effective needs analysis, therefore, requires more than just the systematic collection of information. It involves astute leadership, careful negotiation and an attempt to achieve consensus and commitment in situations where the views and interests of different individuals or groups may not coincide. Experience gained through the project suggests two possible ways in which greater consensus and commitment might be achieved. The first involves appraisal interviewing which has as its main aim, effective staff development. This is discussed in the next chapter. The second possibility involves school-focussed staff development policies, set within an overall LEA INSET plan. This forms the subject of part 3.

5   Needs and the Place of Appraisal/ Staff Development Review

It was mentioned in chapter 2 that all of the pilot schools had, as a result of introducing SFSD policies, moved towards the introduction of some form of appraisal. But why should they have done this and what are the links between appraisal, needs assessment and SFSD? To deal with these questions it is useful, first, to consider the background to the national appraisal debate and the current position regarding schemes already planned or in operation throughout the country. It should then be possible to appreciate what kind of appraisal is most likely to form a part of needs assessment and to fit easily with school-focussed staff development policies.

The Background

Appraisal and Performance Review in Industry

The extent to which appraisal is used in industry, commerce and public administration and the form which it takes is documented in a survey by the Institute of Personnel Management (Long, 1986). Recent thinking tends to divorce appraisal for pay and promotion from 'performance review' and out of a sample of over 300 firms or authorities, 80 per cent operated performance review schemes. These organizations regarded their schemes as having three important purposes: to improve current performance, to set performance objectives and to assess training and development needs. Most carried out a salary review as a completely separate activity.

A noticable trend is to encourage employee participation in the process and to make the interview reports available to both parties. Most of the organizations surveyed now provide training for appraisers. The report also notes that 'ready made systems imported from other organizations rarely function satisfactorily, partly because of organizational cultural differences'. There is an important lesson here for education.

The industrial sector is keen to help education to introduce appraisal. 'Education for Industrial Society' has provided several courses and workshops on appraisal and a series of booklets on management in schools including 'staff appraisal' (Warwick, 1983) and 'target setting' (Trethowan, 1983).

Appraisal for Education: The Government's Initiative

There is little doubt that the government has been influenced by the views and practices of industry in relation to appraisal. Appraisal also forms part of a more general policy which seeks to introduce greater accountability within the education service. Various initiatives such as the setting of aims and objectives, school self-evaluation and an increasing government interest in the curriculum and school organization have resulted in numerous DES and HMI reports indicating the need for teacher appraisal. It was 'sold' badly at first with the 'weeding out' principle apparently behind the Secretary of State's initiative but was eventually redefined through discussion and negotiation with LEAs and teachers' associations.

The publications *Teaching Quality* (DES, 1983) and *Better Schools* (DES, 1985) clearly indicated the government's intention to introduce appraisal. In the latter document it was indicated that the Secretary of State would seek powers 'to require LEA's regularly to appraise the performance of their teachers'. These statutory powers are now available and details of heads' and teachers responsibilities in this respect form part of the government's controversial proposals on *School Teachers Pay and Conditions of Employment* (DES, 1987).

Reactions from the teachers' associations to the idea of appraisal have generally been mixed but in the last two years the issue has become enmeshed in the wider conflict over pay and conditions. Prior to the recent disbanding of the Burnham Committee, and with it the traditional negotiating rights of teachers, the associations were prepared to seriously examine the idea and by 1985 it seemed that most were not opposed to the principle. The problems which remained were those of politics (the pay and conditions problem) resources (how would the costly venture be financed) and detail (the aims and form which appraisal would take).

The ACAS Agreement

The dispute over pay and conditions was referred to the Advisory Conciliation and Arbitration Service (ACAS) and in January 1986 it was agreed to set up a special working group on appraisal/training. Its first report was published in June (ACAS, 1986). Broad agreement was reached on the form which appraisal might take and the preparations which would be necessary prior to implementation. These are some of the main points.

Appraisal should be a continuous and systematic process intended to help individual teachers with their professional development and career planning and also to ensure that the in-service training and deployment of teachers matches the complementary needs of individuals and their schools. It should be related to a job description and should reflect the balance between teaching and other responsibilities outside the classroom.

All teachers, including heads, should be appraised. Each formal interview should be preceded by a self-appraisal and be followed by a written report to be kept by the head and appraisee but to be available to officers authorized by the CEO.

Normally teachers will be appraised by the head, or other experienced teacher designated by the head. The appraisal of heads will be the responsibility of the CEO who will appoint as appraiser an appropriate person with relevant experience as a headteacher.

All teachers should be trained to play their part in appraisal and a nationally endorsed handbook on procedures should be lodged with every school. Resources should be made available for these purposes. The report contains sample documents concerning interview preparation, profiles and target setting which might be used as part of the process.

A pilot study directed by a National Steering Group (unions, LEAs and DES) should be set up. This would involve six LEAs which, in consultation with teachers in their areas, would introduce and monitor appraisal schemes. The end result would be a tested set of documents and procedures which non-participating LEAs would be able to adopt in their areas.

The report, which represented substantial progress, was incorporated, more or less intact, in the so called 'Coventry Agreement' of July 1986. This was signed by the employers and five of the teachers' associations — NUT, AMMA, NAHT, PAT and SHA. Further details still had to be negotiated and there was no agreement on the matter of confidentiality of reports and whether these should automatically be available to officers authorized by the Chief Education Officer.

It was, however, agreed that the pilot project would be launched in 1987. Six LEAs are now taking part but without the support of the teacher associations, most of whom refused to participate due to the continuing industrial dispute.

Previous Experience of Appraisal in Education

In 1985, HMI published the results of a survey involving six LEAs and twenty-one schools *Quality in Schools: Evaluation and Appraisal* (HMI, 1985). The report indicated that at least five LEAs were actively engaged in drawing up appraisal policies and several more were about to follow suit. Also, Butterworth (1986) presents a brief survey of six unnamed authorities. All have initiated trials within their schools and the report concludes that the place of the LEA, as employer, is crucial. 'It must mediate and monitor appraisal, ensuring comparability of methodology and criteria across institutions'.

A scheme to be introduced in Croydon based upon target setting has been outlined by the CEO (Naismith, 1985). Details of the Nottingham approach *Teacher Professional Appraisal as Part of a Development Programme* is also available (Notts CC, 1985). Cumbria has made some progress in introducing a scheme worked out with the teachers' associations. It focusses upon professional staff development and sees individual appraisal as part of whole school evaluation. A pilot study was first carried out involving a quarter of the County's schools and this has now been extended to all schools. (Cumbria CC, 1984).

The DES funded a project in Suffolk and the report 'Those having torches...' (Graham, 1985) provides a useful survey and analysis of teacher appraisal schemes at home and abroad. It points to the advantages and disadvantages of the various approaches used and emphasizes the need to separate review and development from pay and promotion decisions. It places the onus squarely on LEAs for developing detailed policy guidelines in this respect.

But, quite apart from LEA initiatives many individual schools have been practising appraisal for some time. This is confirmed by two reports. A survey, carried out from the University of Bath (James and Newman, 1985), obtained completed questionnaires from over 200 comprehensive schools in the Midlands, South and West of

England. Out of these about 25 per cent were already operating schemes and over 40 per cent were planning to introduce one.

A more detailed Open University survey, *A First Review and Register of School and College Based Teacher Appraisal Schemes* (Turner and Clift, 1985) gives details of schemes in operation in fifty schools. (A second review is due to be published shortly). Most were available to all teaching staff on a voluntary basis. They were mainly designed to facilitate staff development and involved an annual interview conducted by the head, deputy head or a head of department, year or house. Most used a pro-forma completed before the interview by the appraisee. In nearly all cases records were kept of the interview and these were available to the head, appraiser and appraisee only. Most schools reported an increase in in-service work as a result and other benefits such as clarification of responsibilities, improved motivation and curriculum developments.

East Sussex, SFSD and Appraisal

The position at the time the Sussex pilot schools were approaching the task of producing SFSD policies was interesting, confused and changing almost by the month. The teachers' associations, through the ACAS agreement, had given their blessing to a form of appraisal which emphasized professional development, career planning and accompanying INSET activities. They had also agreed to the setting up of national pilot schemes. There were already many examples of appraisal systems in operation throughout the country and a survey carried out by the SFSD project indicated that in 1986, twenty schools in East Sussex already had schemes and fifty-eight more were formulating one. Furthermore, the pilot schools had mostly included some form of appraisal in their SFSD policies and this in most cases either had the full backing of staff or was not opposed by them.

But the national scene kept changing as the negotiations failed to produce agreement and new moves were made by both parties to strengthen their positions. Appraisal became a bargaining counter in the dispute and many people seemed uncertain as to how to handle the matter at local level. In East Sussex the teachers' associations had been kept fully informed about the progress of SFSD and had fully backed the initiative but there was always the danger that they would withdraw their support if they suspected that SFSD was merely a 'back door' to the introduction of a fully fledged 'DES style' appraisal scheme. Some statement from the project team on the subject of appraisal, therefore, became necessary.

A Discussion Document and Its Progress

In 1986 it was decided at senior officer level that, prior to any formal government initiative, a discussion document should be made available to schools, teachers' associations and County advisers for comment. Reactions to the document would then form the basis for further discussion, eventually leading towards a County policy on the issue. The original report was widely circulated and used at several workshops and meetings. It provoked considerable comment and has been revised several times on the basis of feedback from teachers, heads, advisers and teachers' associations. At present it has the status of a document offering guidelines to schools considering introducing staff development interviews within the framework of SFSD. It does not represent County policy on appraisal and is unlikely to progress further until the national situation is clarified.

One important point at issue is whether the process, as part of SFSD, should be called appraisal at all. Eraut (1986) draws a distinction between teacher appraisal and teacher development. The former, he argues, is associated with accountability and demands a major review of performance every five years. This should provide 'an agreed appraisal of performance for the file, which would note the achievements of the previous five years' and provide 'an explicit demonstration of the teacher's and the school's commitment to teaching quality and their continuing desire to improve it'.

If, however, teacher development is regarded as the main purpose of the exercise then an annual staff development interview between a teacher and a head or other senior member of staff is required. This would cover: the teacher's own view of his or her strengths and weaknesses; priorities for developing professional knowledge and skills; and school priorities for staff development arising from proposed curriculum change, school review, developing class teachers' all-round capabilities, etc.

Eraut argues that it is the product which will determine the real purpose of appraisal.

If the product is an action plan for development, then the appraisal interview will become a staff development interview under another name... But if the product is an agreed appraisal of a teacher's performance for insertion into their file, the appraisal foreground will put staff development purposes very much into the background.

Appraisal for accountability, therefore, tends to be retrospective in its judgment and attempts to measure or grade performance against certain norms or criteria. The Suffolk project (Graham, 1985) found various examples of this in other countries. For instance, in some states in the USA it was noted that:

> Many teachers, however, continue to be evaluated by procedures which owe more to the performance review systems of industry than those of education. Whilst teachers expect to be held accountable for the way in which they perform their duties, they are inclined to mistrust a system which, although claiming to improve performance, can be used to facilitate dismissal. Such evaluation instruments, often with vague categories which invite subjective judgments, are straightforwardly summative, offering little or nothing in the way of constructive advice or help, merely reporting on retrospective performance... (p. 53)

Another example is taken from a system in Ontario.

> Procedures and criteria are detailed in the School Board's 56 page manual, 'Guidelines for the Evaluation of Teaching Staff', covering timelines, job descriptions, the documentation and examples of completed forms showing both good and bad performance... Teachers experiencing difficulties (i.e. rated 'unsatisfactory') are placed 'on review', receiving more frequent classroom observation followed by detailed advice, recommendations and supportive action for improvement, all well documented; then, in ordered sequence, a Letter of Concern, which if necessary, is followed by a Letter of Doubt. (p. 48)

Where does the form of appraisal associated with the SFSD project fit with the distinction made by Eraut between accountability and development? This is a question that has created much discussion and has been resolved, for the present at least, by emphasizing the 'developmental' rather than the 'accountability' aspect. This is largely in line with the ACAS agreement and generally has the support of the teachers' associations. There may, however, yet be some hard bargaining on this distinction if the government proceeds with proposals which lean more towards 'accountability'.

With these points in mind the County issued a brief statement which firmly placed the guidelines within the 'developmental' mode and adopted the title *Staff Development Review*

> The staff development review process has as its primary objective the assessment of the personal development needs of individual teachers in order to promote improved learning experiences in the classroom. It includes both self-evaluation and evaluation by a senior colleague, not necessarily the headteacher or principal of the establishment. It should provide individual teachers with opportunities to review their own practice, to discuss strengths and weaknesses in confidence with a senior colleague, and to identify future goals and training needs which will further promote good practice. The staff development review process is separate from any consideration of pay and promotion.

Behind this short statement lies the longer report which is available to all schools in the County. What follows are the main sections of this report which have been modified here first, to take account of feedback and secondly, to avoid repeating matters that have already been discussed in this and earlier chapters. In the light of the points made above, the reader should consider how the following matters are dealt with:

> the separation of staff development review from pay and promotion;
>
> the concept of a joint problem solving approach and the possibility of teacher participation in the process;
>
> the need for comprehensive and accurate information as the basis for the interview;
>
> the importance of a job description and target setting based upon clearly defined responsibilities;
>
> the confidentiality of reports;
>
> the need for each school to devise its own scheme within broad guidelines;
>
> the close links between staff development review and SFSD.

With regard to the last point, the experience of the project schools indicates that there are important connections between SFSD and staff development review. First, as policies are being formulated it is necessary to identify needs systematically and a review is an important and effective way of doing this. Second, if a review scheme is introduced, the interviews will almost certainly indicate problems which require staff development solutions. Without a staff development policy these solutions are less likely to be available. SFSD, therefore, indicates the need for review whilst review highlights the need for staff development. Finally, there is a sense in which the review itself can be considered a form of staff development. For the interviewer it requires skills of a high order, particularly in connection with collecting evidence, questioning, listening, counselling, target setting and motivating. Many of these skills will have to be learned or further developed. The interviewee, also, will have to engage in a process of self-evaluation and thinking through of goals, achievements and future action which are, in themselves, an essential part of professional development.

SFSD, Appraisal and Staff Development Review:
A Discussion Document for East Sussex Schools

Appraisal can serve a multitude of purposes including: checking and monitoring performance, motivating staff, allocating rewards, planning future staffing needs, developing individuals, discovering training needs for the organization as a whole etc. An Open University survey, however, indicates that most schools with appraisal schemes place '*staff development*' as the main aim of their scheme (Turner and Clift, 1985). A similar view regarding the aim of appraisal is contained in the ACAS report on appraisal/training (ACAS, 1986). Furthermore, it is the approach most suited to inclusion within a school-focussed staff development scheme. For this reason the term 'staff development review' is preferred and will be used throughout this report.

Staff development review involves the collection of information concerning all aspects of a teacher's work and the provision of suitable opportunities for this to be discussed in the light of prevailing circumstances. It should lead to the identification and implementation of an agreed development plan on the part of the teacher and supportive action by the interviewer.

Focus

Staff development review might focus upon all or any of the following depending upon a person's role within a school:

teaching skills;

relationship with pupils, staff and parents;

curriculum development;

professional development;

extra curricular activities;

managerial and administrative skills.

Some schemes rely upon target setting which may be set for any or all of the above and are usually related to objectives for the coming year. They are usually concerned with specific tasks (for example, making one's science teaching more activity-based, introducing a new syllabus for third year history, organizing an in-service programme, introducing a new organization structure).

It is recommended that schools consider all of the above but that the possibility of establishing a few clear targets each year, for each individual, should be given serious attention.

Information

Satisfactory review requires adequate information. This might be obtained from a variety of sources, for example:

questionnaires or other forms to be completed by the interviewee;

any other information volunteered by the interviewee;

classroom observation — by interviewer or other member of staff;

information regarding the conditions under which the interviewee has been working (for example, lack of resources, difficult groups, especially difficult tasks);

interviewers own general knowledge of the individual's work.

We recommend that as much evidence from as many sources as possible be used in conjunction with job descriptions and targets (set in previous interviews).

Interviews

On the basis of industrial experience, reports from schools with existing schemes and discussions with the staff of pilot schools in East Sussex the following recommendations are made:

(i)   Interviews should normally be held once each year and both parties should be properly prepared. Pro-forma statements should be completed beforehand. Other evidence (from reports, classroom observation etc) should be available, together with the job description.

(ii)   The interview should allow a two-way exchange of views on jointly recognized problems. The person interviewed should provide evidence concerning his or her own needs for staff development but these will be set in the context of the needs of the school or department by the interviewer. The interviewee should also be encouraged to comment upon the degree of support received in carrying out his or her work.

(iii)   The interview should concentrate upon an analysis of whatever aspects of the teacher's work (or derived targets) are appropriate, rather than upon characteristics of the individual. It should emphasize development (what needs to be done for improvement) rather than deficiencies in performance.

(iv)   At the end of the interview an agreed statement should be prepared setting out the action to be taken by both parties before the next interview. The interviewee should have the final say concerning to whom the report should be made available.

Issues for consideration

The following have been identified as areas of concern and are dealt with in turn.

(i)   Style of scheme
(ii)   Acceptance of scheme by staff
(iii)   Cost
(iv)   Skill training
(v)   Expectations and follow up

Style of scheme   In some schemes the head does all the interviewing. In others it is delegated to deputy heads, to heads of departments, to head of year or, in some cases, to any person or persons chosen by those appraised. This spreads the load but it may have attendant problems, for example, lack of coordination, variable quality of interviews, widespread training needs etc. Also, who should interview a teacher for subject work, tutor work, whole school contribution? Lack of credibility of some 'line managers' may sometimes spoil schemes based upon neat, hierarchical patterns.

It is clear from the Open University survey (Turner and Clift, 1985) that types of scheme will be influenced by institutional factors such as size of school, organizational structure, management style, existence of formal school plans and policies etc. For instance, it may be possible in a small school with centralized leadership for the head to conduct all interviews. In a large school with an established participative decision making structure this may be neither possible nor desirable.

Another problem is who should interview the head? The following procedures have been adopted by different schools. The head has been interviewed by: a head of department in whose department he/she teaches and by the deputy heads, separately or together; a specially selected panel of staff; by another head or a retired head, possibly assisted by one or more staff from the school or by advisers/inspectors sometimes accompanied by someone outside of the education service such as a manager from industry. There are many possibilities.

Decisions made with regard to the style of the scheme are clearly a matter for each school to work out for themselves. From a staff development point of view, there are advantages in the interviewer being sufficiently senior to be able to take whatever action is necessary to help the interviewee achieve agreed targets. Nevertheless, until further experience of different approaches has been gained, it is recommended that any scheme that might eventually be adopted County-wide should have sufficient flexibility to allow for institutional preferences.

Acceptance Trust and confidence will have to be built up and this may take time. It is recommended that:

> any proposed scheme be discussed fully with staff and their views be taken into account in devising and implementing the scheme;

> participation be voluntary in the first instance. It is assumed, however, that those who have assisted in drawing up the scheme will be willing to take part in and help to improve it.

Cost The minimum time for an interview is likely to be one hour but there will be at least another one-and-a-half hours for preparation and follow-up action. Furthermore, if the recommendations of the Suffolk Study (Graham, 1985) are to be adopted, further time will be necessary for interviewers to observe the teaching skills of those to be interviewed.

The time of the person to be interviewed must also be considered. Preparation for the interview, the interview itself and follow-up activities will add up to several hours (at least) per person.

It is recommended that the costs be carefully considered before a County-wide scheme is proposed.

Skill training   The training of interviewers also involves cost, not only of provision but of time. There are two aspects: interview skills and classroom observation skills.

Interviewing involves many activities (for example, listening, negotiating, target setting) and personal attributes (for example, sensitivity, perceptiveness). Some of these may be possessed by interviewers already, others may not. Some training will be necessary, at the very least to raise awareness of the problems likely to be encountered and to give some practice in interviewing. In order to gather relevant information, the interviewers may also need training in classroom observation skills.

It is recommended that the county consider how such training might be supported within its annual INSET programme.

Expectations and follow up   There is a close relationship between review and staff development. A scheme will lose credibility if ideas and expectations (especially those related to career development) raised during interviews are not followed up.

It is recommended that schemes form part of a school-focussed staff development policy in each institution.

The Next Stage

It seems likely that all schools in the county will include some form of 'staff development review' as part of their SFSD policy but this will be for each school to decide for itself. For the present, pending the outcome of the ongoing dispute on pay and conditions, the document will stand as a discussion paper embodying a set of voluntary guidelines for schools wishing to create their own schemes.

Some might argue that using the term 'staff development review' rather than appraisal merely side-steps a difficult issue. But this view can be countered by two points. First it offers a way forward in the present, difficult situation in which appraisal, carrying with it connotations of accountability, is unlikely to produce commitment on the part of those appraised. Secondly, it may in the long term prove to be the most appropriate way of building trust and confidence enabling other aspects of performance review to be considered from a solid background of experience and knowledge.

Summary

Appraisal has here been distinguished from staff development review. The former is primarily concerned with past performance and accountability and the latter with the future development of the individual and the school. School-focussed staff development requires the careful analysis of needs and an important way of obtaining information in this respect is through an annual staff development interview. The pilot schools in the SFSD project found this a valuable and, in most cases, necessary aspect of their policies. A report on the links between SFSD, appraisal and staff development review was prepared by the project team. In it, the annual interview is regarded as a joint problem solving exercise. Its primary purpose is to consider the staff development needs of the individual within the context of those of the school. The discussion which takes place should result in a plan of action for the coming year to which both parties are committed.

Part III
Policies: Possibilities and Problems

The assessment of staff development needs was considered in Part II. Part III now turns to policy construction.

The meaning of the term policy and the reasons for having a formal document are dealt with first followed by some suggestions as to how to create an effective policy statement which involves and engages the interest of staff. This is followed by a detailed analysis of the key elements of a policy and examples of policy documents drawing upon the work of the pilot schools to illustrate the various points made.

Finally the whole question of SFSD policy making is set within the wider context of an LEAs INSET plans.

6 Creating a Policy

In this chapter, a case will be made for every school and college to have its own written, staff development policy in the form of an easily understood, freely available, document. The meaning of policy will be discussed first, followed by the case for a formal, policy statement. Approaches to the task of drawing up a policy will then be considered.

The Meaning of Policy

Ask most people — what is policy? — and the response will normally be that it has to do with intentions or with current practice. 'It is our policy to do this or that' they will suggest by way of example. But further elaboration is usually difficult and confused. This is not suprising as policy is a word which, like 'curriculum' and 'evaluation', for instance, is used often and loosely and seems to have several meanings.

Hogwood and Gunn (1984) have analyzed the many different ways in which the term is used in relation to government policy and listed below are the main ones, to which are appended examples from SFSD policies (in italics) which indicate how that usage might apply to schools.

1 As a label for a field of activity, for example, economic policy or foreign policy. In the case of a school — *The School's staff development policy.*

2 As an expression of a general purpose or desired state of affairs, for example as in a party manifesto: 'In the next parliament, we shall endeavour to bring inflation lower still'

> — *The overriding aim of this policy is to enrich the curriculum for pupils through the full professional development of the capacities and expertise of all staff.*

3 As a specific proposal for example to give union members the right to hold ballots — *A staff development file will be kept for each member of staff which will be accessible only to the head and the member of staff concerned unless otherwise agreed between them.*

4 As a formal authorization such as a government directive — *A requirement that all members of the teaching staff have an annual staff development interview.*

5 As a programme in a specific sphere of activity involving a package of legislation, organization and resources, for example, a housing policy — *The use of TRIST funding (resources for training allocated by the Manpower Services Commission), for example, for staff development related to the improvement of information technology applications within the school.*

As demonstrated above, the various uses of the word 'policy' apply just as much to schools as to government and it is, therefore, important to be clear as to the meaning of the term in the present context. Jenkins (1978) explores some of the many definitions of policy and considers their usefulness. He shows how it might refer to aims, structure, activities, resources, outputs and outcomes or some or all of these together. Drawing upon his ideas, it is possible to suggest a definition suitable for the purpose of school-focussed staff development.

Policy is:

a set of interrelated decisions
relating to a particular issue or area of activity
concerning the selection of goals
and means of achieving them
over a period of time.

Each of these points needs some clarification. First, a policy is concerned with a set of interrelated decisions. This implies both deliberateness and complexity. We are not dealing with a single vague thought that something might be done but with a conscious commitment linking together several formal decisions.

Secondly, these decisions should relate to a policy area which will normally be defined by the policy statement. Thus, in the present situation, the area is 'school-focussed staff development' and although some people will understand what it means, the policy document should help to remove uncertainties.

Thirdly, a key element in a policy document will be a statement of goals or aims which provide an ongoing sense of direction. There will often be an overriding aim and several supporting or subsidiary aims.

Fourthly, there is a need for details of how such goals might be realized. A policy will be of little use if the goals are not achievable by those involved. Thus the policy should indicate what activities will be undertaken, by whom and using what resources.

Finally, the policy should indicate the planned time during which it is intended to carry out activities and evaluate their outcomes.

The ways in which these elements of policy might be expressed in written form are considered in detail in the next chapter.

The Arguments for and Against a Written Staff Development Policy

The case for having a written statement of policy in every school and college can be made quite forcefully but, first, it is worth considering whether there are any disadvantages. Those listed below, like the advantages referred to later, have emerged from discussions with project members and others involved in devising a staff development policy for their own school.

Policy Can Exist Without it Being Formally Stated

People sometimes say — 'that is (or is not) the way we do things around here' and it is quite probable that their colleagues will agree with them despite the fact that the matter has never been formally discussed or written down. There is, in effect, a policy which has evolved over time, much like the norms of behaviour that grow up in any group. It is, therefore, quite possible that many schools actually have an implicit staff development policy, although one that has never been deliberately thought out, and formalized. But it is suggested here that this is not a satisfactory state of affairs and that much can be gained by examining the assumptions and expectations which people believe to be guiding their actions.

Clear and Comprehensive Policies are Impossible to Attain

Braybrooke and Lindblom (1970) use the phrase 'disjointed incre-
mentalism' to describe what they regard as a normal and reasonable
approach to policy making. They maintain that policy makers mostly
have to operate in confused and uncertain situations with limited
knowledge. They seldom have clear goals and are generally trying to
move away from unsatisfactory situations by trial and error taking
small steps at a time. They also suggest that policy making is usually
uncoordinated; there will generally be many people all 'chipping
away' at the same problem.

They argue that this form of policy making is inevitable where
clear goals and consensus are not possible, where only a few limited
moves are realistically, feasible and where exact outcomes cannot be
predicted. Critics of formal staff development policies may agree that
this is the situation in which many schools now find themselves and
that policy making can only take place using a 'disjointed increment-
alist' approach. This would, however, now be disputed by those
schools in the SFSD project which have prepared policies. Most
would regard this as a negative and defeatist attitude and argue that it
is possible to gain a reasonable level of consensus and plan sensibly for
future action in this area — even in the present difficult working
climate.

*A Written Policy may Inhibit Flexibility and Prevent a Rapid
Response to a New Situation, Particularly if all Resources are
Already Committed*

There is certainly a danger that this could happen and policies should
always be planned and worded in such a way as to allow some room
for manoevre. All resources need not necessarily be tied to specific
programmes. Intentions can be expressed in certain areas leaving final
decisions to be made when more information is available.

*To Draw up a Policy Properly Requires Considerable Time,
Particularly if all Staff are to be Involved in the Exercise*

Drawing up policies is time consuming and if LEAs expect it of their
schools and colleges some time must be made available. In general,
though, those involved in the project felt that policies were of suf-

ficient importance to warrant a reordering of priorities with the need for a staff development policy coming high on the list.

> *Implementing a Staff Development Policy is also Costly.*
> *How can this be Justified in a Time of Financial Constraint?*

For heads and teachers feeling the effects of financial restraint the problem is very real and enthusiasm for a policy will not be strong unless LEAs are prepared to provide additional resources for each institution based upon their individual policies. The cost implications of staff development policies will be considered in more detail in later chapters.

Clearly there are problems and pitfalls to be overcome. Policy, inadequately thought out, poorly explained to staff and badly resourced could prove worse than no policy at all. But if the dangers are anticipated and steps taken to gain the understanding and commitment of staff, the advantages of a having a policy can more than outweigh the possible disadvantages. Here is a list of benefits drawn up by SFSD members

A Focussing Device

The preparation of a policy brings the attention of management and teachers to the subject of staff development.

A Form of Organizational Analysis

In order to prepare a policy it is necessary to analyze needs, both of the school and the individual members of staff, and to order these according to priority. This, in itself, is a valuable exercise and various approaches were described in chapter 5.

A Direction Finder

A policy requires a clear statement of aims together with a rationale for those aims. Schools and their staff will benefit from thinking through and reconfirming these from time to time.

School Focussed Staff Development

A Coordinating Mechanism

A policy brings together, in one coherent statement, disparate plans and activities related to the area of staff development focussed on the school. This can help to avoid overlap and encourage individuals and groups to plan according to the resources available.

A Form of Commitment

To state clearly what is intended indicates a definite commitment to a course of action. This can be reassuring to those affected by the policy. If commitment is shown and the details communicated to those interested then a policy document can form the basis for accountability. The question — 'has it been implemented effectively'? for instance, can be asked by staff, management, governors, pupils and parents.

An Instrument of Communication

Those involved in staff development or affected by what goes on will have a clearer understanding of their rights and responsibilities in this connection.

A Framework for Coping with Change

Schools and colleges are having to change rapidly and often dramatically. Many of these changes require staff development and a policy which indicates aims, priorities and programmes can provide valuable assistance for those responsible for innovation.

Furthermore, LEAs must also cope with change and meet requirements for statements regarding their own INSET policies as set out in DES Circular 6/86. Planning towards this end is considerably helped if each school and college has analyzed and communicated to the LEA its own needs in the area of staff development.

In making the case for staff development policies, it can also be argued that to have an effective policy is both a right and a duty of all staff. They have a right to expect a policy from which they can benefit but they also have a responsibility to contribute towards planning and implementation. Furthermore, it is a right of all pupils. As the beneficiaries of education within the institution they have a vested interest in the quality of teaching and management. Ultimately, staff development is for their benefit. Management in all schools should, therefore, be responsible for ensuring a fair and effective approach to staff development. As proof that this exists there should be a comprehensive policy statement available to all staff.

This is an impressive list and it has generally been enough to convince any doubtful participants in SFSD training programmes. But many of these benefits will depend upon how the idea of a policy is introduced to staff and how it is prepared.

Managing the Process

Without initiatives on the part of a head, head of department or other post-holder the assessment of staff development needs and the drawing up of a policy are unlikely to be carried out. So what is involved and what should be considered in undertaking the task? From the experience of the SFSD team the following conditions are regarded as important.

(i) Preparation
(ii) Presentation
(iii) Participation
(iv) Planning

These conditions do not amount to a recommended sequential path but rather to a simple model indicating important aspects of the policy making process which, if given due regard, should improve the final outcome.

Preparation

It is almost a cliche now to say that the head or other person responsible for introducing change should first create the right climate. What this generally means is that individuals and groups likely to be affected should be open to ideas and ready to listen to the possibility of change. Some schools seem to have this climate already and would probably agree that it has been built up over a period of time based upon conditions of trust and support. If such conditions exist the task will be easier; if they do not then preparation is all the more important. What is involved is some very careful ground-work on the part of the head or person responsible for introducing the policy to ensure that the idea is properly understood and its implications clearly appreciated.

First, there are the values which underlie the change. In the present case these relate to the acceptance of regular reviews of staff development needs and to the actions and activities which become necessary as a result. It can be argued that such reviews and actions should be part of normal professional practice but, in reality, this is generally not the case. Preparation, therefore, must involve a careful analysis of the way the values or ideals associated with the change fit, or do not fit, with the prevailing ethos of the school.

There is also a more pragmatic aspect to consider involving time and resources. To try to innovate with ill-formed ideas which create waves of anxiety and anticipation and then to realize that the scheme cannot be adopted because it is well beyond the resources available is clearly not the best strategy nor the most effective use of time. Preparation is, therefore, essential and thinking through the implications will lead to the next question — how should it be presented to staff?

Presentation

The way the ideas are communicated to staff is also an important element in the change process. If the philosophy and values implicit in the change fit well with those of the school, presentation may be less crucial as it will be seen by staff as an extension of existing ideas and practices. Where, however, the proposed scheme runs counter to these, both the values and resource implications will have to be carefully and fully explained. There are two requirements for this — good, clear information, and time. The procedure should not be rushed and details should be freely available. In this way presentation is likely to become a natural part of the next condition — participation.

Participation

Change can be pushed through with very little consultation and may work — up to a point. What is lost in the top down, authoritarian approach is a sense of ownership and commitment on the part of those affected. Instead of adoption we have adaption and this can progress to such an extent that original intentions are lost. Elliot-Kemp (1986) is emphatic on this point.

An imposed system will, at best, gain compliance; at worst resistance and sabotage. Schools need commitment from staff for any significant change — compliance is not enough. One of the very few certainties we have from the findings of educational research is that when teachers really believe in something they will make it work. (p. 5)

One example of such research is that carried out by Berman and McLaughlin (1978).

Teacher participation in decisions concerning project operations and modifications was strongly correlated with effective implementation and continuation. The reasons for this powerful effect were easy to uncover. Teachers, who are closest to the problems and progress of project activities, are in the best position to suggest remedies for perceived deficiencies. Moreover, where project activities and objectives reflected significant teacher input, the staff were more likely to invest considerable energy needed to make the project work. (p. 29)

Fullan (1982) suggests that participation involves negotiating new meanings with those involved; a process which requires a continual refinement of original ideas. He puts the case as follows:

Do not assume that your version of what the change should be is the one that should or could be implemented. On the contrary, assume that one of the main purposes of the process of implementation is to exchange your reality of what should be through the interaction with implementers and others concerned. Stated another way, assume that successful implementation consists of some transformation or continual development of ideas. (p. 91)

Thus, for those introducing SFSD, whatever their position in the hierarchy, the message is clear. Involve staff in decision making concerning the planning and implementation of the change.

Planning

Preparation, presentation and participation are all part of the planning process and underpin it. Detailed planning involves asking and answering key questions such as: when should a start be made? Who will be in charge? How many people should be involved? What exactly will they do? How long should it run? Should it be phased? What resources should be made available? How should it be monitored? etc.

It is worth heeding another of Fullan's (1982) warnings here: 'Assume that effective change takes time. It is a process of "development in use". Unrealistic or undefined time-lines fail to recognize that implementation occurs developmentally'. In the present context, this warning means that an effective policy cannot be introduced too quickly — it requires time, patience and sensitivity.

The sense of participation is all important. If the programme emerges naturally from discussion and negotiation then it will have more meaning for those involved. The programme itself may well be tentative and uncertain and may involve trials or pilots and further discussion before something more substantial is accepted. Certainly, the idea of phasing in a new system in managable steps is one that should not be overlooked. Too much, too soon, can easily destroy good preparatory groundwork. Whatever kind of programme emerges it should be clear to those involved what is happening and why. A clear written statement setting out this information is recommended and should form a basis for ongoing discussion, monitoring and development.

This then is the background to the introduction of formal SFSD policies and indicates the important role of management in the process. New ideas can and should come from those with leadership roles. As suggested in chapter 5, those having such roles may be in a better position to forsee needs as distinct from wants. The overall, longer term, view must be clearly presented to staff and be open for discussion. An important aspect of leadership is the ability to convince others that important, not easily recognizable, change is necessary.

There is now a considerable literature on the management of change and innovation strategies and references have been made to various authors in the above discussion. However, a recent contribution to this field — *Making School-centred INSET Work* (Eason, 1985) — should be particularly helpful to those introducing SFSD policies. It not only identifies the issues involved in introducing INSET activities into a school but also provides helpful strategies and procedures for gaining support and commitment.

Summary

Policy has several meanings but is taken here to mean:

a set of interrelated decisions relating to a particular issue or area of activity concerning the selection of goals and means of achieving them over a period of time.

It will be shown in the next chapter how this definition underpins the SFSD policies produced by the pilot schools.

The main advantages of having an SFSD policy are that, it acts as:

(i)   A focussing device (on staff development).
(ii)   A form of organizational analysis (requiring the assessment and ordering of needs).
(iii)   A direction finder (requiring a statement of aims).
(iv)   A coordinating mechanism (bringing together disparate staff development activities).
(v)   A form of commitment (to SFSD).
(vi)   An instrument of communication (regarding SFSD).
(vii)   A framework for coping with change (encouraging pre-planning in the area of staff development).

If the support and commitment of staff is to be gained it is important to consider carefully four key conditions in introducing and drawing up the policy. These are: preparation, presentation, participation and planning.

The experience of the project team indicates that the more that staff are involved in the creation of the the policy the more they are likely to be involved in its implementation and further development.

7 The Elements of a Policy

In this chapter it will be shown that a policy normally contains a number of key elements. As members of the project produced draft policies for their schools these were analyzed by the team as a whole and it became clear that several aspects were important and kept reappearing in the documents. They were: aims and rationale; structure (including the assessment of needs); programme (including, activities, costs and timing) and evaluation. These will now be considered and illustrated in turn with reference to the policies produced by the team. The exact wording has sometimes been altered in order to make sense of extracts taken out of their full context.

Aims and Rationale

The aims will inevitably be set in the context of the school or college but they will often be justified in relation to a more general rationale. The following is a rationale for a policy prepared by a primary school.

> It is essential that we continue to grow in professional stature and experience backed by the support of a comprehensive programme of in-service opportunities designed to help all of us to meet the growing demands with confidence, a sense of purpose and, as can be the case, an increased personal job satisfaction. Positively-planned Staff Development (SD) is a means of satisfying these considerations...

This rationale then leads into the following statement of aims.

Overriding Aim

The continuing development of the curriculum experience of pupils through the enhancement of the professional skills and qualities of the staff.

Supporting Aims

(a) To enable individual staff to commit themselves to their own professional development while enabling management to accept responsibility for implementation.
(b) To provide experience likely to contribute to a career structure.
(c) To recognize and employ staff strengths.
(d) To provide a means of identifying staff needs.
(e) To create development conditions and professional awareness.
(f) To foster the search for best practice.

These aims and rationale might be compared with those put forward in a secondary school policy.

Meaning of SFSD

What is staff development? A staff development programme is a planned process of development which enhances the quality of pupil learning by identifying, clarifying and meeting the individual needs of the staff within the context of the institution as a whole. The programme has three strands relating to the individual, interest groups and the whole school.

Why school-focussed? Because it moves professional development from being something 'in addition', to a part of the life of every teacher and every school. It recognizes the specialized needs of each member of staff and their professional potential in contributing to developmental activities. It demands more relevant design of INSET experience to meet needs and avoids reliance on the general 'course'. It provides a useful forum for curriculum continuity and innovation across traditional subject boundaries and it involves all staff in the development of the school as well as sharing responsibility for their development.

Aims of Staff Development

The primary aim of staff development is to increase the quality of pupil learning by the development of staff potential. Subsidiary aims are:

(i)   To recognize and employ staff strengths in seeking the best teaching practices.
(ii)   To identify staff needs.
(iii)   To provide experience and guidance likely to contribute to career development.
(iv)   To make professional development a right and duty of all staff, and the responsibility of management and the LEA.
(v)   To create the most favourable climate for ensuring the continuance of staff development.

Should the aims and the rationale be so detailed? The SFSD team became convinced, particularly after consulting colleagues in each school, that careful explanation was a necessary part of the policy making process. This should involve discussion and negotiation as a preliminary step but should be followed by the embodiment of the outcomes in a formal statement of the kind shown above. This also has the advantage of providing clear guidelines for incoming members of staff not involved in the early stages of negotiation.

Structure

Structure, as set out in a policy, defines roles and responsibilities in connection with the identification of staff development needs and with the implementation of the programme and evaluation of its outcomes.

In most schools, the head or other senior members of staff will have a prime responsibility for initiating and overseeing the policy-making process, but many of the actual tasks involved will be delegated to individuals, committees or working groups. Some excerpts from the policies will make this clear. The first is from a primary school where an opening statement explains the leading role of the head.

1   *Consultation process.* The implementation of staff development will evolve through a process of consultation with the whole staff.
2   *Staff meetings.* Staff meetings (held at least fortnightly)

provide the forum through which all can make a contribution to the development of the school. A pattern of
business meetings at lunch times and curriculum meetings
after school will be used.
3 *Head.* The head will have a key role to play as coordinator
of staff development, recognizing that professional development is a right and duty of all staff, and its implementation a responsibility of management. The deputy
head will assist the head in this task.

The next excerpt is from a secondary school in which one of the
deputy heads takes the main responsibility.

The policy will be reviewed at the end of each academic year
and priorities for a programme for the next academic year will
be agreed upon in consultation with the whole staff, through
the existing meeting structure.
    The formulation of the staff development policy is
through consultations with the whole staff, the governors and
the local education authority. This will be coordinated by the
deputy head with responsibility for staff development.
    It will be the responsibility of the coordinator to:
1 ensure that the process of consultation is continuous
throughout;
2 staff are fully informed on policy matters and that there are
opportunities for comment and contributions from all
colleagues (this includes non-teaching staff);
3 arrange for the collation and dissemination of information
relating to staff development;
4 monitor staff development initiatives;
5 review priorities for initiatives;
6 allocate available finance evenly;
7 be accountable to the head, and through the head, to the
governors for the working of the policy.

The next excerpt is from another secondary school and is more
complex. SFSD throughout the school is coordinated by a special
committee.

One member of the committee will be elected from each
faculty and the committee will elect its own chairman. Should
the group prove to be predominantly senior staff the committee reserves the right to coopt other interested staff.
    The committee will meet twice a term and two changes

of personnel at least, and four at most, will take place each year.

It is suggested that in the first year the head should contribute by sharing the results of the (SFSD) project but that later he would be available to be coopted onto the committee as necessary.

The staff development committee will have the authority to develop the policy and recommend priorities thus enabling it to function as a powerful advisory group within the school.

The committee, which is accountable to the management team, is given a mandate which requires it to: collate and disseminate all information relating to staff development; create a programme; establish priorities for the following year having received information from individual members of staff, whole staff meetings, curriculum and progress meetings and the management team; receive initial requests for secondment and advise on availability and attendance at short courses etc; advise the management team on the programme planning for in-service days; allocate finances for SFSD and review the policy and the programme annually.

These excerpts indicate that quite different approaches can be taken on the structural aspects of policies. In general, these will tend to derive from the established management style in each school. The following approaches, which depend upon the main location of authority for decisions in connection with staff development, were identified in the SFSD project.

A   'Head'. The head assumes full responsibility but consults with staff.
B   'Deputy'. Another member of staff, usually a deputy, accepts responsibility but is accountable directly to the head.
C   'Committee'. A committee is set up with elected or selected representatives to take overall control of staff development but to report to the head or management team.
D   'Departmental'. A committee is set up to coordinate the programme but major responsibility for needs assessment and policy implementation is delegated to departmental heads.
E   'Staff'. The staff as a whole act as the decision making body through regular meetings which may be chaired by any member according to the topic being considered. A staff development coordinator will act as secretary to the meeting and ensure adequate circulation of information.

These approaches might be combined or modified or they may change over time but what has been learned from the Project is that there is no single structure that will meet the needs of all schools and colleges. The approach adopted is very much a product of the normal decision making process and expectations within each institution. There will normally be one person (perhaps called a 'staff development co-ordinator') who has responsibility for overseeing the process. This person may act in his or her own right or through a group or committee but will be accountable for ensuring that the intentions of the policy are followed through whatever mechanism has been agreed. They will, thus, generally, carry more authority than the 'professional tutor' envisaged by the James Report (DES, 1972).

Programme

The programme sets out details of the specific activities which will take place within the policy framework. These are sometimes linked to the responsibilities of various people or organizational units. It will also give details of the timing of the activities and their cost. A policy statement of this kind provides a means of coordinating existing activities (which some schools may have engaged in for some time) with new initiatives which may have been discussed but not carried further.

Chapter 2 contained details of the SFSD, pilot school programmes and further examples are set out in the illustrative policy documents in chapter 8. By way of comparison, and to add variety, some of the possibilities identified in the Schools Council Project — *School-Based Staff Development Activities* (Oldroyd, Smith and Lee, 1984) are set out below.

Whole School Activities

Career counselling for staff
The staff library
Dissemination of information on external courses
Adapting staff meetings for INSET
Staff conferences

School Focussed Staff Development

Activities for Existing Groups

Induction of new staff
Visits to other schools
Links with feeder schools
Developing tutorial skills
Job enrichment and rotation of
  tasks
Academic and pastoral team
  review

Using management meetings
  for INSET
Use of external course activities
  for school-based INSET
Staff development for senior
  management
Inter-school INSET activities

Interest Group Activities

Staff study groups and seminars
School-based courses
Self-regulating staff
  development groups
Become a pupil for a day
Cooperative teaching

School-based remedial INSET
  group
Using broadcasts for INSET
Exchange of teachers
Mutual lesson observation.

Many of these activities are included in the SFSD policies and have been tried over the past two years. In the programme, all that may be necessary is a brief statement of the activity concerned such as:

In-service Days

Topics for the in-service days each year, their format and timing will be decided at the staff development meetings as arranged.

Links with Playgroups

The reception teacher will visit playgroups in the village so as to forge closer links between them and the school.

A slightly longer statement may sometimes be necessary giving some details of the procedures to be adopted for instance:

Job Descriptions

Each member of staff will have a detailed job description worked out through initial discussion with the head covering essentially their organizational responsibilities within the school. Job descriptions should be reviewed annually when changes will be made if necessary. The head or teacher concerned may also seek to renegotiate the job description at any time.

Some schools have felt it necessary to explain procedures in even greater detail in the policy document and two examples are included here to illustrate how this might be done. The first is taken from a primary school policy and illustrates the way in which the programme fits with the structure and practices of the school. It operates an open plan system and, as far as possible a flexible timetable. These notions are embodied in the policy statement and related to staff development activities.

Timetable Flexibility

The 'open primary school timetable' should be used to full advantage in developing the skills and techniques of staff. This can be achieved in the following ways.

(a) Provision will be made to enable colleagues with special curriculum responsibilities to work alongside others in order to promote the subject areas concerned, adding expertise to the teaching situation to boost confidence and provide on the job training.

(b) Provision will also be made for a class exchange situation as a regular feature of the timetable, involving those with special responsibilities or expertise (for example in creative English, science or religious education). This will be of benefit to the children who will gain from the different approaches and to the staff who will have the opportunity to broaden their experience of other age groups in the school.

(c) Mutual classroom observation between pairs of colleagues will also be arranged after discussion with the head on details of the scheme.

(d) There will be ongoing consultation between the head and staff to ensure timetable flexibility in order to achieve (a) (b) and (c) above.

Another example is taken from a secondary school policy.

Job Enrichment and Rotation of Tasks

Routine and particular tasks will be annually examined by departments and by the standing committee with a view to providing opportunities for staff to engage in job enrichment activities. Individual teachers are invited to request of the head or the head of department experience of a new task in order to broaden experience, increase the level of involvement within the department or school and add to their job satisfaction.

The following are some of the possibilities:

> Joining the time-tabling team, the reading group, working parties or school committees; departmental responsibilities such as stock control and running examinations or shadowing senior colleagues.

It is possible to include all kinds of activities within the programme but those drafting policies should bear in mind that if the contents are to be regarded seriously by staff the programme must be seen to be feasible. This involves a consideration of timing and costs.

Timing

Timing is an essential part of any policy. Only so much can be achieved in any one year and it is, therefore, necessary for policies to make clear not only what is intended but also when the various activities will take place. Those responsible for drawing up a policy will generally find it necessary to establish priorities and to state these in the written document. As the time horizon extends, however, the statements of intent may necessarily be less precise and more conditional. It is assumed that through the regular review and evaluation of the policy it will be updated and more detail and precision will be added to 'future' statements as the time approaches.

By way of example, one secondary school accepted the need for an appraisal scheme, as part of its staff development policy but saw this as a future commitment which required careful research and negotiation. The policy was worded as follows:

> The Staff Development Committee, in consultation with the staff and the unions should examine the most positive way of developing staff development review scheme in the school. This section of the policy needs much examination, clear objectives and further training in interviewing skills and techniques...

A pilot scheme, with some time made available, could be operated with senior staff and volunteers in the summer term of 1986.

This illustrates the nature of policies which, basically, express intentions and commitments. The level of detail can vary considerably and as a general rule, those activities which will require action in the near future will be stated in a more precise way than those which are planned for the more distant future.

This has implications for the actual layout of the policy document. There may be certain activities which it is intended should be ongoing and form the basis of the programme. The example of job descriptions mentioned above assumed this role in one of the SFSD primary schools and mutual classroom observation played the same important role in another. These will normally be included in the main part of the document. But it is likely that either the details of the activities (for example, the number of staff taking part or the time devoted to the scheme) or other, less permanent, activities will vary from year to year. In this case it is sensible to have a detachable sheet containing a detailed summary of the programme for the coming year. This will provide important information for all staff within the school and for the LEA officers in drawing up the annual INSET budget as explained in chapters 8 and 9.

Costs

We are concerned here mainly with costs to the schools themselves. The wider implications of SFSD policies for the LEA will be considered later. The project schools agreed that it was possible to deal with costs under three main headings.

1 Existing staff development activities for which no call has previously been made, or will be made, for extra resources.
2 New activities to be undertaken, again without the need for additional resources. Examples from the various policies under both of these headings include for instance:

induction and weekly tutorials for student teachers and new staff; school and departmental meetings specifically for staff development; departmental reviews; staff library; school/industry liaison; some courses run by staff for other staff, for example, on computers; career counselling by the head; providing formal feedback to colleagues on INSET activities;

job rotation and exchanges of responsibility; teacher exchange, liaison or cooperative ventures with another school.

The pilot schools agreed that the amount of activity which could be undertaken within a limited budget would depend upon their being able to generate some extra time and the following suggestions were made.

Schools should:

(i) review organization and management routines and practices to establish whether time might be found for new priorities in the area of staff development;

(ii) consider the use of staffing allocations and whether savings might be made and devoted to SD activities;

(iii) review the use of post-examination time in the summer term;

(iv) make more efficient use of ancillary staff and new technologies to relieve the administrative load on teachers and school management.

The extent to which these reviews are carried out, and time is generated as a result, relies upon the goodwill of the management and staff and the degree to which staff development is seen as a priority. Clearly, the necessary goodwill may be lacking in many schools at the present time and will depend upon the outcome of discussions over pay, conditions and negotiating rights. A more recent variable in the time equation is the proposed introduction of the so called 'Baker days'. This alludes to the five non-teaching days referred to in the government's proposals on pay and conditions (DES, 1987). It is assumed by many that all, or some, of these will be used for INSET activities.

3 New developments with additional costs attached. Even the most creative use of time will not provide the resources necessary for much school organized staff development activity and here additional resources will be required. It is the costing of this work which will provide the school with its annual earmarked staff development budget. Examples from various budgets are shown below.

(i) Mutual classroom observation scheme. Twenty days supply cover £1200.

(ii) Other school/further education/industry visits. Twenty-five per year. Supply cover £1500.

(iii)   Travelling expenses for visits £300.

(iv)   Fees and expenses for visiting speakers £200.

(v)   Release time for staff to engage in staff development consultancy work with colleagues. Supply cover £400.

(vi)   Release time for staff development coordinator. Supply cover £600.

(vii) Expenses for staff library directly linked to professional reading group within school £450.

It is clear that the kind of items which might appear under this heading will vary according to the priorities of the school but that much of the money claimed will be for supply cover for the release of staff from the classroom. This is to be expected as much staff development work will involve teachers in activities which, by their nature must take place during school time.

Non-school Organized Activities

There will continue to be INSET work planned, implemented and funded outside of the school. Such activities may be centrally initiated, or offered by LEAs through advisers or teachers centres or by providers of long and short courses such as universities, polytechnics colleges or industrial or commercial concerns.

The costs of these will not fall on the schools themselves but will, nevertheless, need to be considered by the LEA in its annual budget. Schools will, therefore, be required in their policy statements to make clear whether they have plans for allowing members of staff to attend certain courses or whether they would wish the Authority to consider providing, or negotiating for, specific provision. It is in this area of policy formulation that close liaison is required between schools and LEAs on a regular basis. Coordination and forward planning in terms of Authority and school policies is a prerequisite to successful INSET provision in the future. This is a matter that is considered in more detail in chapter 9.

Evaluation

One of the main arguments levelled against written policies is that all too often they become mere bureaucratic encumbrances which add to the paper stored in the school office. In other words the policy becomes an end in itself rather than a means of achieving effective staff development. This is, indeed, a hazard but one way to overcome the problem is to build in a regular review and evaluation procedure.

The pilot schools have taken different approaches to this but all have allocated responsibility to a person or committee for collecting evidence and reporting back, with conclusions, to the staff each year. Information is usually sought through the use of questionnaires or interviews and seeks to establish whether individuals have taken part in the programme, the benefits to them as a result, their views on the extent and nature of the programme provided and ways in which they feel it should be modified in the coming year.

If regular evaluation of this kind is formalized and accepted by staff it should help to create the idea of policy as 'living' and evolving aspect of school life rather than a static and inflexible instrument of management. If properly worded and organized, policy becomes a means of encouraging and facilitating necessary change as against a sterile and unyielding set of rules and procedures which might inhibit innovation. The evaluation scheme, therefore, is an important component of any policy.

Summary

This chapter has outlined the main parts of a policy statement. A useful acronym for the elements is ASPECT

A -ims
S -tructure
P -rogramme
E -valuation
C -osts
T -iming

Together these should provide sufficient detail to enable staff to understand what is intended and how the policy aims will be achieved. It is stressed that a policy is no more than a means to an end and that implementation, evaluation and modification should be an ongoing process. Furthermore, the continual review and updating of policies will be required by the LEA as part of its overall INSET plan.

8　Examples of SFSD Policies

This chapter contains three sample policy documents which are set out in full in order to provide as much information as possible for those responsible for drawing up policies in their own schools. They contain a considerable amount of material which illustrates all aspects of a policy statement. Each comprises extracts from the policies of several schools and thereby represents the combined experience of the growing number of schools in the SFSD scheme. They are intended to illustrate different approaches to policy formulation and drafting and the different priorities which underpin the resulting programmes.

There is a debate amongst the heads of the fifty or so schools involved so far as to whether policy documents should be brief and fairly general or full and detailed. Those supporting the former view argue that a long document will not be read and that too much detail inhibits flexibility. Those holding the opposite viewpoint argue that their staff both need and appreciate the explanation and detail contained in a longer document and that a full and comprehensive statement is useful both as a reminder to existing staff as to what has been agreed and a help to incoming staff who were not involved in the original discussions.

The County has agreed to provide guidelines giving an overall framework within which policies should be written but the length and style of the schools' policy document will be left entirely to each school provided there is sufficient information available for monitoring and budgetary purposes. The guidelines, which will be given to the representatives of each school during SFSD training workshops are as follows.

Policy Outline

The policy will normally contain several distinct parts. These are set out here with a brief explanation. What you put in each section is entirely for you to decide on the basis of discussions with staff. The sections need not be in the order set out below but it is suggested that you end with the costed programme which should always be on a separate sheet or sheets.

Aims

These should be set in the context of the school. Do you have an overriding aim such as the following?

'The continuing development of the curriculum experience of pupils through the enhancement of the professional skills and qualities of the staff'.

Do you have supporting aims? 'To recognize and employ staff strengths to best advantage' is one sometimes used but most policies have several.

Structure

Structure, as set out in a policy, defines roles and responsibilities in connection with the identification of staff development needs and with implementation and the evaluation of policy outcomes.

In most schools, the head or other senior members of staff will have a prime responsibility for organizing staff development activities, including the analysis of needs, but many of the actual tasks involved will be delegated to individuals, committees or working groups.

Whatever style you use it will be necessary for you to be clear as to who should do what and when. If a committee is set up then spell out its constitution and brief.

Programme of Activities

The programme sets out what will be done in the name of staff development within the school. It provides details of the specific activities which will take place. It will normally be updated each year. The following headings are taken from several policies and no one school has included them all.

1   In school courses/workshops.
2   Special support programmes, for example, for student teachers, probationers or others.
3   Mutual support, for example, through classroom observation, collaborative teaching, reports on courses attended etc.
4   Problem solving groups set up to look at particular issues.
5   Better communication, for example, by producing a staff handbook, an SD noticeboard, a staff library, etc.
6   Job experience through sharing tasks, standing in for another etc.
7   Reviews, for example, through job descriptions, open files, career interviews, appraisal etc.
8   Visits/exchanges.
9   External courses.

Evaluation

Policies documents can easily become just part of the paperwork. One way to overcome this is to build in a regular review and evaluation procedure and to attach specific responsibility to a person or group for carrying it out. Who will you appoint and what questions will they ask of whom? Who will they report to?

Costed Programme for Coming Year

This should be set out on the form provided and show:

1   Existing staff development activities which do not involve additional cost.
2   New developments involving no additional cost.
3   New developments with additional costs attached. These activities will provide the school with its annual SD budget.

For example — autum term: travelling expenses for visits to × schools — £100.

spring term: release for teacher to engage in staff development consultancy work with colleagues. Supply cover — £200.

This information is required by March each year so that agreement can be given for implementation in April. An additional form will be required in July setting out the needs identified and the proposals for area, County or national courses in the following year. The area general adviser will collate all proposals by 1 June in order to reach the County INSET group by 1 July. This information will form the basis for the adviser's programme for the following year.

Within these broad headings it is expected that there will be considerable differences between schools in actual content and detail. The following documents illustrate the possible variety. The first is one that might have been produced by a small (three teacher) rural primary school. This has been included because there are many such schools and the argument was originally advanced by some heads in the county that as teachers in these schools normally know each other well there is hardly a need for a staff development policy. The experience of the project has proved this to be incorrect and has shown that much can be gained through preparing and implementing a policy. It has also been included to indicate how a local federation of small schools might work in relation to staff development in order to overcome the problems of small scale. It will receive a budget of £300 (a minimum figure for small schools) from the County.

The second is a policy that might be used by a medium/ large primary school. For the sake of accuracy in costing we will assume a full-time staff equivalent of fourteen teachers which will provide an annual SFSD budget from the County of £840. Because of the number of teachers it is possible to make a fair proportion of the programme school-based.

The third relates to a comprehensive school and illustrates the additional complexities involved as more sub-units are included. It is assumed that there are sixty staff producing an annual SFSD budget of £3600.

Readers who intend, eventually, to draw up their own policies should be selective in choosing parts of these documents to suit their own ends and should, preferably, work out their own wording with staff from the school concerned.

A Policy for a Small School

Introduction

It is recognized that much of what goes on in this school already might be classified as staff development. The purpose of the policy is to clarify our aims in this respect and to focus on priorities and ways of achieving our goals. Being a small school with only three members of staff we must try to look outside for stimulus, experience and help. The policy identifies ways in which this might be done.

Aim

To improve the quality of the education of the children who attend the school by identifying and striving to meet the professional needs of the staff individually and collectively in the context of the whole school.

Structure

The head will take overall responsibility for drawing up and implementing the policy but there will be full consultation with the assistant teachers and the final document will represent a consensus on all issues. Regular staff meetings will take place after school (at least once a fortnight) to discuss and decide upon:

1   needs and priorities for staff development;
2   details of the annual programme;
3   monitoring and review of the programme;

and also to undertake staff development activities.

As much of our staff development work will take place alongside the four other schools in our local, small schools federation further meetings will be required on a monthly basis to discuss the above points with our colleagues. The first of these has already taken place and the outcomes are reflected in the programme below.

Programme

The success of our policy will depend upon the good relationships that already exist between members of staff and our proven ability to work closely together. We should endeavour to build upon and extend this situation in every way possible. But in drawing up a policy for such a small group we must also focus upon possibilities outside of the school and make full use of the potential offered (a) by our small schools federation; and (b) by the County and elsewhere. The programme is therefore in two parts indicating internal and external activities.

Internal activities

(i)   Teaching as a team — we already operate as a team in most teaching activities but it is our intention to utilize to the full, existing and extra resources (including supply cover paid for under SFSD, head's non-teaching time, timetable flexibility and any voluntary assistance available in the classroom) to enable team teaching, mutual classroom observation and regular class exchanges to take place.

(ii)   We will meet formally at least once a fortnight for one hour to discuss developments and decide upon what further steps might be taken to extend cooperation and experience within the school. We will enlist wherever possible the help of the advisory service in this respect.

(iii)   Although we know each other very well the head will arrange a formal staff development interview each year to review each person's career, their progress and that of the school as a whole. This will take place during the summer term and will focus upon the year's work including achievements and difficulties. Ways of overcoming problems will be considered. Targets will be set when this seems appropriate and the information stemming from the interview will form the basis for planning the staff development programme for the coming year.

The head will be interviewed annually by two other heads from the small schools' federation.

External activities

(i)   An exchange of teachers scheme has been agreed within the federation. This is on a voluntary basis but all of us in this school are committed to the idea and visits have been arranged for the coming term.

(ii) A joint workshop on an agreed topic will be planned each term by the five federation schools. These will sometimes use annual in-service closure days and sometimes be arranged after school. On occasions speakers from outside of the teaching force (including parents, governors, the county support services or any member of the community who may be able to impart knowledge or skills not otherwise available to us) may be invited to speak.

(iii) Visits will be arranged each term to other schools within the County where it is felt there are things we can learn.

(iv) The head will take responsibility for advising other members of staff of any courses which may be appropriate for one or more persons to attend and it will be our joint responsibility to identify areas where it is felt that the federation or County might be encouraged to provide courses. Areas identified so far include: science/environmental studies, expressive arts and reading/language.

Evaluation

It is important that the outcomes of the policy are kept under review. The head will produce a report each year for discussion by staff. It is also the intention to exchange reports with the federation schools.

School Based Programme 1987/88

Existing activities (at no extra cost)

Use of in-service days.
Career discussions with the head.
Class exchanges.
Some classroom observation.
Occasional visits to local play groups.

New activities (at no extra cost)

A series of three science support courses at teachers' centre to be attended by two staff.

An extension of the classroom observation scheme.

Three, teacher exchanges with other schools in the federation (length of time to be agreed).

New activities to be funded via SFSD in priority order

Supply cover to 'top-up' mutual observation and team teaching scheme — £120
Cover to release staff for annual review interviews — £60
Half day visits to other schools: cover and travel — £70
Outside speakers' fees (contribution to federation workshops) — £50
Total £300 (max)

Area/county courses identified as needs in priority order 1988/89

Science/environmental studies.
Reading and language.

(these would extend the work already being undertaken within the federation schools)

National and regional courses identified as needs in priority order 1988/89

One member of staff to attend a course on expressive arts in the primary school. She has a particular interest in this area and if allowed to attend could act as consultant within the federation.

The head to attend a twenty-day management course at the University.

(Note: The next two policy statements cover a wide range of activities and are possibly more extensive than would be necessary for any one school. Also the details of various schemes such as mutual classroom observation, staff development review, the programme for student teachers etc. are set out in full. Some policy makers might prefer to refer only briefly to such schemes in the policy statement and to provide full details for staff in separate documents. But for the purpose of the present exercise, which is to provide as much information as possible to would-be policy makers, it has been decided to include the wording in full.)

A Policy for a Medium/Large Primary School

Introduction

Staff development is seen as 'all planned activities directed towards improving the professional knowledge, skills and capacity of teachers whether organized at the school or elsewhere'. Such activities should in the long term help in the development of the school and its staff as well as improving the education of the children.

Staff development has always been a continuous process in the school but a written policy will be a means of encapsulating all existing and new staff development activities within the overall aims of the school. It will identify the needs and priorities for staff development through the pooling of ideas as well as providing greater agreement on the roles of individuals. All staff will be involved in the construction and operation of the policy.

Aims

1   To draw together the disparate aspects of staff development within the school and to provide the opportunity for adding further activities as appropriate.
2   To improve professional standards.
3   To provide opportunities for individuals to further their careers.
4   To increase job satisfaction.

5   To increase team work.
6   To improve the educational opportunities of the pupils.

Structure

The staff as a whole is the decision-making body for staff development. Regular meetings will be held after school to discuss and decide upon activities and schemes, the allocation of resources, review and evaluation of the policy and its programme and the planning of future programmes.

Fortnightly meetings will be held throughout the year between 3.45 p.m. and 4.45 p.m. on days when no school clubs take place. Attendance will not be obligatory. An agenda will be prepared and distributed to all staff.

The purposes of the meetings will be: to ascertain staff development needs by whatever means are agreed; to oversee the working of the staff development policy; to agree its programme and activities; to review and evaluate the policy and to provide and arena for some staff development activities to take place.

Different people will chair the meetings according to the topics under discussion. A smaller group, consisting of senior members of staff plus any other teacher directly involved may meet on an occasional basis to consider specific issues and report to the full staff later.

Time will be made available for staff development activities and planning through:

(i)   voluntary sessions after school, on a regular basis;
(ii)   reallocation of timetable periods where possible to accommodate activities during the school day;
(iii)   additional resources from the LEA

Roles

Head

Oversee the operation of the policy and the allocation of resources. Validate the programme. Participate in the annual review of staff under the agreed scheme and reach agreement on individual job descriptions. Maintain the 'open files' of staff under the provisions of the scheme set out later and ensure their confidentiality. Provide a counselling facility for staff.

Deputy head

Participate in the review of staff under the agreed scheme. Assist in the running of the various other schemes and activities set out in the policy. Attend staff development meetings.

Year leaders

Help to ensure members of the year are informed of and able to participate in the various activities. Attend staff development meetings or delegate this task to another suitable member of the year group.

Staff development coordinator

Be responsible for collecting information regarding staff development needs and preparing a draft programme on the basis of this. Ensure adequate circulation of information concerning the various schemes and activities within the policy. Act as secretary at the regular staff development meetings, preparing agendas and summarizing outcomes for all staff. Offer advice on current staff development activities both in the school and in other establishments. Ensure that the policy is reviewed annually and draw up the amended document each year.

Post-holders

Coordinate their particular area of responsibility throughout the school and act as curriculum or staff development consultants as and when appropriate.

All staff

Participate in the operation of the policy, its evaluation and review and the setting up of the annual programmes. Provide information for colleagues on return from external courses where this is seen to be useful.

Needs

In the first instance, staff development needs will be identified through interviews which the head will have with each member of staff; through a whole school questionnaire (based upon the GRIDS scheme) and through reports from each year groups representative prepared after discussion with members of their year group. From this information the head and staff development coordinator will prepare an outline programme for discussion by the whole school committee.

Programme of Activities

Open file system

Each member of staff will have a file, accessible only to the head and the teacher concerned. Information from this file will not be disclosed to any other person without the express permission of that teacher. The contents may include:

(i) Job description — see below.

(ii) Details of courses attended. It will be the responsibility of the individual to see that these details are properly logged.

(iii) Copies of any documents produced by the teacher for the information of colleagues after attendance at external courses.

(iv) Copies of papers produced by the teacher for the use and benefit of colleagues concerned with, for example, his/her curriculum or organizational responsibility.

(v) Administrative letters concerning the teacher, considered to be important by the head or teacher concerned.

(vi) Notes on mutual lesson observation carried out according to the school scheme (see below);

(vii) Review statement completed in accordance with the school scheme (see below).

Job descriptions

In the early part of each academic year all members of staff will negotiate with the head to complete a detailed job description to an agreed format, covering organizational responsibilities within the school. Individuals will first complete a document for the head who will then accept it or negotiate additions or deletions. The head or teacher may seek to re-negotiate the job description at any time.

The final, agreed document will be placed in the open file referred to above. All or part of the job description may be used to provide information to other members of staff and to obtain a clear indication of the overall organization of the school. It will also be used in the staff development review scheme.

External courses

When members of staff attend an external course they will decide whether or not the outcomes are of sufficient interest or importance to be reported to other members of staff. They should be prepared to write a resume and circulate it to all staff. They should also be prepared to offer further information at a special staff development meeting which may be called by the SD coordinator. A copy of the resume or details of any SD session provided should be added to the teacher's open file.

Mutual observation scheme

There are two main reasons for operating a mutual observation scheme: (i) to improve teaching skills; and (ii) to promote curriculum change. The object is not to look for weaknesses but to share problems with a view to finding solutions. It is unlikely that the whole staff could participate in the scheme in any one year and priorities will have to be agreed during the regular staff development meetings.

The following ground rules have been agreed. Two teachers will select each other for mutual observation of at least one lesson (or part-of-lesson) each. One or more preliminary discussions will take place in order to agree on a specific teaching skill or classroom aspect which each will observe in the other's lesson. The mode of operation will also be decided, including the nature of note-taking and reporting back in follow-up discussions.

Strict confidentiality between the two participants must

be maintained unless they both agree to share their own experiences with others. What use is made of the outcome of the observation will depend upon the nature of the aspect(s) observed. Some agreement may be made between the participants that either or both will engage upon a plan-of-action which may require a further observation session later. Other sessions may result purely in discussion. Whatever records or notes are made, it will be the decision of the individual concerned whether or not to include them in his/her open file.

It is advisable that information on the possibilities surrounding classroom observation is sought from the staff development coordinator and/or from suitably experienced colleagues before the preliminary discussions.

Counselling

The head will be available to discuss career matters and/or professional development with any member of staff. The discussions may include, how best to use the contents of the open file, knowledge of interview procedures or what particular schools may be looking for, shared ideas on strengths to offer etc. A 'de-briefing' after an interview, whether successful or not, will also be offered and should be useful for future applications.

If not applying for another post elsewhere in the immediate future or if not considering applications at all, a member of staff may wish to discuss possible means of widening experience within the school.

Staff development review

Time will be made available for members of staff to have a one-to-one interview with either the head or deputy head on a voluntary basis. The head will be interviewed by the deputy head. The deputy may nominate another senior member of staff as her own interviewer if so wished.

Four fundamental principles will be observed:

(i)   the statement prepared after the interview must be arrived at jointly, with both parties in agreement;

(ii)   the contents of the statement will be confidential to the teacher and the head (also the deputy head if

involved), unless the teacher agrees to specific discl-
osure;

(iii)   the object of the interview is to identify strengths
        and weaknesses and to discuss needs and direction
        for future continuous improvements i.e. to provide
        a springboard for further professional development;

(iv)   the participants should eventually be trained in
        interviewing skills and techniques.

The interview will take the form of a discussion of how
both parties perceived the year's work - which were the particular successes, failures, etc and why? Classroom teaching
and special responsibilities will be considered. Any problems
or difficulties identified will be analyzed and possible methods
of overcoming them suggested together with targets for the
forthcoming year. The following year's possibilities for the
individual, both in personal career and in his/her role within
the school will also be discussed.

The statement, set out on an agreed format, should contain the main points of the interview and details of any plan of
action. Each statement will be referred to during the following
year's interview but will be destroyed after two years.

Further details will be agreed during the regular staff
development meetings, with a view to the first interviews
taking place in the summer term of 1986.

Induction scheme

For probationary staff — Opportunities and invitations will be
extended for preliminary visits during the summer term prior
to taking up of appointment. The year leader concerned will
take first responsibility for ensuring that adequate information
is given for carrying out the tasks assigned and the normal
day-to-day class administration. Teachers with posts of responsibility will also make themselves available to explain
their roles. The head will maintain overall responsibility.

Preparation/assimilation time will be made available to
the probationer where possible. He or she will be given priority when resource time is allocated, both for observation of
other teachers and for the mutual observation scheme. Opportunity will be given for staff development interview(s) during
the year if desired.

For newly-appointed staff — The same areas of responsibility will apply as for probationary staff. Newly-appointed teachers will not necessarily have priority on resource time but some time should be made available for assimilation into the new environment, particularly at the beginning of the appointment.

For supply staff — The degree of induction will depend directly upon the length of service the individual is expected to supply. For short-term supply teachers it will be very limited but build up as more regular contact with the school develops.

In-service days

Topics, format and timing for the INSET days each year will be decided at the staff development meetings.

Information

For all categories of induction and for the general use of the whole staff, it is envisaged that by the beginning of 1986 a school information file will be available. The following information will be provided in an easily accessible form:

Staff list and their respective responsibilities.
School rules.
Equipment available for use.
Calendar of typical year's events.
Details of school day to include timings, playground duty operation, lunch time procedures, assembly procedures.
Library use.
Details of PTA and governing body.
Any other information considered useful.

Communications regarding staff development

Apart from staff development meetings, other means of communicating information on this topic will be through bulletins in the weekly information envelopes and space allocated on the noticeboard. The staff development coordinator will summarize the business of the meetings and circulate this to staff.

Further possibilities

The following suggestions for possible inclusion in future programmes will be considered by the Staff Development Committee.

Visits to other schools — If resources are available, some teachers many find it valuable to visit another school in the area, for example, the local infants school or secondary school.

Rotation of responsibility — Some areas of responsibility may be amenable to change from one member of staff to another, thereby increasing experience. The possibilities of regularly changing year groups could be investigated.

Short courses — Interested members of staff may wish to run or participate in short course after school, for example, interviewing skills, mutual observation techniques, displaying work.

Evaluation and Review/Forward Planning

An annual evaluation and review process will be carried out, probably in the summer term, for the purposes of determining the effectiveness of the policy and the year's programme. The review should consider the policy's value to both individuals and groups of staff and to the school as a whole.

From the evaluation and review procedure, alterations to the policy may be made. The recommendations will be of value in the preparation of the following year's programme produced through collective agreement. The staff development coordinator, or other nominated member of staff will be responsible for making a record of the full proceedings and producing a synopsis for colleagues.

School-based Programme 1987/88

Existing activities (at no extra cost)

In-service days.
Induction programme.

INSET course feedback to staff.
Careers counselling.
Exchange of responsibility.

New activities (at no extra cost)

INSET/staff development meetings held fortnightly after school.

Production of school information handbooks out of capitation.

Head's time during review interviewing or standing in for deputy head whilst interviewing.

Head's time substituting for teacher engaged in mutual classroom observation (NB, this covers only part of cost).

Year group and whole school reviews.

Teacher exchange between schools.

Time of staff development coordinator.

Extension of some existing SD activities ie. INSET feedback and induction programme.

New activities to be funded via SFSD in priority order

Visits to other schools to study particular curriculum areas or to liaise with infant/secondary schools. Duration — half day. Estimated six visits plus travel expenses — £200
Staff development interviews. Time for staff release. Fourteen staff × 1.5 hours — £200
Mutual observation. Four pairs. Time required to prepare, observe and report — £360
Visiting lecturers in connection with INSET workshops — £80
Total £840

Area/county courses identified as needs in priority order 1988/89

Interviewing skills for SD review.
Mutual classroom observation skills.
Discussion groups on making the best use of supply staff.

*National and regional courses identified as needs in
priority order 1988/89*

Curriculum evaluation and whole school review.
Management course (for deputy).
Records of achievement.
Children with special needs.

A Secondary School Policy

Introduction

The intention of a school-focussed staff development policy
is to provide a planned programme which will enhance the
quality of pupil's learning by identifying, clarifying, and meeting the individual needs of the staff within the context of the
institution as a whole.

It is called school-focussed because it moves professional
development from being something 'in addition', to a part of
the life of every teacher in the school. It seeks to recognize the
specialized needs of each member of staff and their potential in
contributing to developmental activities.

The intention of this policy is to focus attention on the
aims, structure and activities of staff development in the
school. Though outside support and resources will be forthcoming, the initiatives, commitment, goodwill and employment of talent must come from within. The place of staff
development within the context of the school can be represented by a simple model.

Figure 1

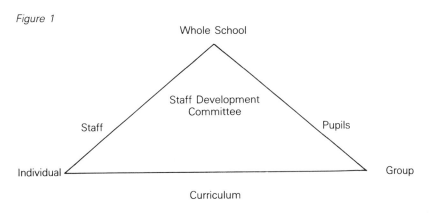

119

The three corners of the triangle represent the main parties to the staff development policy — signifying individual, group and corporate rights and responsibilities in the process. The three sides represent the main elements involved in the process of learning — the pupils, the staff and the curriculum. A policy must ensure that the parties and elements, as shown in the model, are fairly represented in the process of decision making and the activities which take place as a result.

Aims

Overriding aim

To increase the quality of pupil learning by the development of staff potential.

Supporting aims

1   To make professional development a right and a duty of all staff and a responsibility of management.
2   To provide experiences likely to contribute to the personal and professional development for each member of staff.
3   To coordinate individual and whole school in-service education and training in order to respond to the needs of the school in the search for best practice and to meet the challenge of change.

Structure

A standing committee for staff development (SDC)
    The SDC will be drawn from all departments and one member will be elected from each. The head will also be a member. If the elected group is mainly senior staff, the Committee may coopt interested junior staff. The Committee will elect its own chairperson. It will meet twice a term and two changes of personnel will take place each year on a rolling basis. The mandate given to the Committee is:

(a)   To collate and disseminate information relating to staff development using all appropriate channels of communication.

(b)   To receive information regarding needs from individual members of staff, the curriculum committee, faculty and other interest groups, whole staff meetings and the management team.

(c)   To establish priorities and draw up an agreed programme each year.

(d)   To prepare a budget and to allocate resources to the various activities.

(e)   To delegate tasks as appropriate in connection with the planning and implementation of staff development activities.

(f)   To advise the management team on the programme for in-service days or other school-based courses or workshops.

(g)   To advise the management team on requests for secondments or for attendance on courses other than those lasting for less than five days or taking place out of school hours. In addition the SDC will assist the management team to draw up, each year, a list of courses or other activities which the school feels should be supported by the County. This list might include for instance:

    (i)   existing courses provided by the Polytechnic or University or other training establishment;

    (ii)   courses, programmes or workshops on particular subjects that should be provided or arranged by the County;

    (iii)   the names of members of staff who would wish to attend such courses;

    (iv)   any other activity that would be of interest to the school but would be beyond its capacity to provide within the limits of its SFSD budget.

(h)   To review the policy and the programme annually in the light of reports received from all sources.

(i)   To report to, and be accountable to, the management team.

Minutes of all meetings will be posted in the staff room for a week before being filed.

(a), (b) and (c) above relate to the identification and collation of needs for staff development. The committee will, from time to time, decide upon the most appropriate ways of obtaining and dealing with such information. The following are possibilities:

whole school reviews — these may be undertaken using INSET days for meetings of whole staff and/or by the use of questionnaires;

departmental, house, year or other group reviews organized by the head of unit;

staff development, career or other interviews with individaul members of staff provided the information from such interviews is made available by those concerned;

reports of any kind relating to, for instance, curriculum reviews, examination results or external developments which will place new demands on the school;

information offered, or requests made, by any member of staff at any time.

The Programme

The aims of the policy are extensive and it will not be possible to achieve most of them for several years. The plan is, therefore, to create a rolling programme in which certain activities are intended to lead to short-term objectives whilst others envisage a longer time horizon.

The programme is divided into three parts:
the first relates to initiatives originating at school level (from the SDC or the management team);

the second concerns those initiatives stemming from a functional or interest group (such as a department or year group);

and the third is for those initiatives which come from individual members of staff.

School level initiatives

Staff INSET conference days — Full use will be made of the two days permitted annually by the LEA when the pupils do not attend school. The programmes will be devoted to a specific theme, drawn up and prepared in advance by the SDC in consultation with staff and the management team. The day may involve visiting lecturers, staff speakers, discussion groups, departmental meetings, workshops and/or plenary sessions.

Other in-house courses — From time to time, as needs are identified, the SDC will organize short courses or workshops. Departments, interest groups or individual members of staff are requested to suggest areas or topics for consideration by the SDC.

Staff documents — The following documents contain important information. They will be reviewed annually by the SDC and provided to all staff.

(a) The Staff Diary/Work Book
(b) The Staff Hand Book

Library facilities — Limited funds are available from library and departmental capitation and from funds administered by the SDC. Staff are invited to recommend titles to the Librarian.

The following documents are generally available. HMSO. publications, Schools Council working papers and copies of the *Times Educational Supplement*. Copies of every departmental syllabus. Details of external courses (a copy will be available in the staff room for one week before being placed in the library).

Staff can also make use of the Education Library at Sussex University and the Polytechnic Library at Falmer. Details can be obtained from the staff librarian.

Career counselling — The SDC will set up a careers service for staff, offering guidance on jobs available, help with CVs and letters of application and interviews.

Working parties — Occasionally, working parties concerned with specific problems affecting the school as a whole will be set up by the management team or the SDC. Any member of staff may be invited to join the team according to interest and experience. This is considered to be a valuable staff-development activity.

Group initiatives

Departments — Departments are responsible for encouraging their own staff development including cooperation in the planning, teaching and evaluation of work, arranging visits to other schools, developing skills for mutual lesson observation and analysis, attendance at in-service and school-based courses and involvement in external examination boards and subject committees.

The head of department will be responsible for organizing:

(a) regular departmental meetings with published agendas and minutes;

(b) departmental in-service meetings, courses or workshops;

(c) working parties concerned with matters of direct concern to the department;

(d) the work of probationary teachers in the department in liaison with the probationer's teacher tutor;

(e) the work of the student teacher in liaison with the school tutor with special responsibility for student teachers;

(f) involvement of the LEA advisers in discussion of plans and problems.

Each department will prepare its own staff development policy to be submitted to the SDC by April each year.

Pastoral groups — The pastoral committee will meet twice a term and agendas and minutes will be published. Any member of staff may be invited to join the committee when topics of particular interest to them are being discussed. The committee will organize school-based courses on pastoral issues as the need is identified.

Upper and lower school meetings will also take place for all form tutors twice a term, with dates published well in advance. Heads of upper and lower schools with their year tutors will be responsible for encouraging the development of pastoral skills and the organization of tutor time. Special meetings will be called by the heads of upper and lower school for staff involved with particular groups. Year tutors will organise activities for their year group.

Liaison with feeder primary schools, sixth form colleges,

technical colleges, careers officers and employers will be maintained and extended and opportunities will be offered for those interested to join the pastoral team on visits.

Termly meetings will be held with the primary schools to discuss current needs and interests. Heads of department, subject advisers and other staff particularly involved will be invited.

New Staff — A programme will be organized by the school tutor. This will normally include a meeting in the summer term to familiarize new teachers with their surroundings and to meet colleagues. This should be arranged with the head of department. During this time the teacher should be given the school handbook and diary, a personal timetable and an explanation of pupil groupings, syllabus requirements, room locations and availability of resources.

An 'induction programme' will be published at the beginning of each term for all new staff. The teacher tutor and head of department will meet the new teachers on the day before the start of their first term and explain duties, form list, registers etc.

Regular meetings will be held in the autumn and spring terms to further explain the organizational structure of the school and encourage discussion of problems arising in the first year of teaching.

The teacher tutor will meet probationary teachers weekly during morning tutor time to discuss specific problems and evaluate progress. Throughout the probationary period, the teacher tutor and head of department will be available to give guidance, visit lessons, and discuss reviews of performance.

Student teacher — The student teacher's timetable, pastoral involvement (attached to a form tutor) and evaluation of work is organized by a student's tutor (normally a senior teacher). The tutor will liaise with the Polytechnic and University regarding student placement and organize all administration, teaching practice and the assessment procedure.

The tutor will meet students on a regular basis to discuss problems or difficulties and provide them with the opportunity to observe lessons taught by experienced staff. The tutor will also arrange a meeting in the summer term for heads of departments who wish to involve a student in their department in the following academic year.

Each student will also be attached to a year tutor throughout their practice and will attend registration and assembly with that tutor.

Heads of departments will arrange for students to observe lessons and familiarize themselves with the daily routine of the department. They will also discuss lesson preparation and arrange for teaching to be observed regularly, followed by discussion.

Supply teacher — It is expected that the number of supply teachers working in the school will increase. A member of staff will be given specific responsibility for contacting them early in the term and for creating a package of information to ease and facilitate their work. A welcome 'tea' will be offered in September for those interested in supply work.

Individual initiatives

External courses — These will be published on the notice board in the staff room or sent directly to staff. Applications for courses involving absence from school for longer than five days must be made to the head. For other courses, the initial contact should be with the head of department and then with the chairperson of the SDC. A form obtainable from the head's secretary, must be completed to obtain supply cover and expenses from the LEA.

Preparation is necessary for most courses and feedback will be expected on return. As a minimum, a brief report should be completed and handed to the secretary of the SDC for display or distribution. The SDC will decide with the teacher concerned whether he or she should be involved in further follow-up activities. All attendance on courses during school time will be published on the staff notice board together with the name of the course.

Teacher exchange — Provision is made by the LEA for long or short term teacher exchange within the County. Teachers interested should discuss proposals initially with their head of department and the chairperson of the SDC.

Job enrichment and rotation of tasks — Individual teachers are invited to request the head or their head of department for experience of new tasks (for example, chairing committees, organizing examinations, timetabling etc.) in order to broaden their experience and add to their job satisfaction.

Mutual classroom observation — Teachers may ask for assistance in arranging this from their head of department or from the SDC or they may make their own arrangements with colleagues. The value of the exercise lies in observing others and being observed, followed by constructive feedback. The SDC has some useful materials and video-tapes illustrating the process.

Visits to other schools or to industrial/commercial establishments — Requests to carry out visits should be made to the chair person of the SDC. The application should in all cases receive the backing of the head of department concerned.

Other activities — Staff are encouraged to undertake any activities which they feel might benefit them in their work or careers. If resources are required then the SDC should be approached but in any case a report on such activities would be welcomed.

Staff development review — This is included as an individual activity for several reasons. Although it will almost certainly involve at least one other person and may eventually be organized on a more formal basis, for the time being it will be voluntary and regarded as a right of each teacher within the school. It is the intention of the school to seek training for several members of staff in the skills necessary and eventually to provide school-based training. On an experimental basis, however, the head and two deputy heads (all of whom have themselves been interviewed) will be prepared to interview any member of staff. More details of this entirely voluntary scheme will be posted on the staff room notice board in due course.

Evaluation of the policy

The Staff Development Committee will actively seek feedback before updating and modifying the policy each year. Members will be required to obtain information as to:

(i) Whether the policy has correctly identified the needs of the school;

(ii) Whether staff have benefitted professionally during the year as a result of the policy;

(iii) What evidence there is that change has taken place in response to the operation of the policy.

The SDC will be responsible for collecting and analyzing information of this kind both formally and informally. An evaluation report will be submitted to the management team each year.

Costed Programme

Additional resources will be available from the County and in order to obtain these a detailed costing based upon parts of the programme set out above will be necessary each year. The programme for next year is detailed below.

School-based programme 1987/88

Existing activities (at no extra cost)

Induction and weekly tutorials for student teachers and new staff.
Professional guidance and counselling by head and deputy.
Job rotation.
Staff and departmental meetings for INSET.
School and departmental reviews.
Working parties.
School/industry/FE liaison.

New activities (at no extra cost)

Courses for non-teaching staff.
Specific task experience.

Teacher exchange.

Flexible use of staffing to employ half a post for staff development activities.

New activities to be funded via SFSD in priority order

School visits, five days cover and travel — £350

Providing induction conference for new staff — £600

Mutual observation scheme, ten days supply cover — £600

Additional industrial visits; travel costs only — £250

Workshop on SD review and interviewing skills for all staff. Visiting lecturer's fees etc. — £200

Time for review interviews, approx 120 hours — £1200

Materials for updating staff library — £150

School based courses for typing, computers and word processing. Visiting tutor's fees and expenses — £150

Total £3500

AREA/County Courses identified as needs in priority order 1988/89

Career counselling.

Interviewing skills for staff development review.

Use of computers for administration.

Student centred learning.

Records of achievement and profiles.

Modularization in the curriculm.

Health related fitness.

National and regional course identified as needs in priority order 1988/89

Management courses for heads of department.

Managing school finances under the LMS scheme.

Curriculum evaluation.

Curriculum development especially relating to pre-vocational courses; BTEC, City and Guilds.

Career counselling for senior pupils.

A list of those interested in applying for these courses will be supplied separately after further meetings of the staff development committee.

Summary

Three examples of hypothetical staff development policies were set out in full; one for a small primary school, one for a medium-sized primary and one for a fairly large comprehensive. These policies, in their present form, have not been used by any single school but each represents and amalgam of ideas from several SFSD schools. They are meant to illustrate various possibilities for those intending to draw up their own policiies. Costing is shown and is important as part of the 'bid' process for SFSD funds from the County. The final part of each document, indicating priorities for external courses, is also important in helping to determine the county's INSET plan for the coming year(s).

9 Some of the Wider Implications of SFSD: One LEA's Response

As LEAs begin to follow more closely the spirit and conditions of DES Circular 6/86, schools will increasingly be required to assess their own needs for staff development and produce schemes for meeting them. The way this might be done and the case for written policy statements was discussed in earlier chapters. But the problem now arises — how should an LEA which follows the SFSD route deal with the information flowing in from several hundred schools? Circular 6/86 offers some advice in relation to the INSET proposals which each authority must submit to the DES annually.

> The Secretary of State will wish to assure himself that these proposals are related to systematically assessed needs and priorities, are set within balanced and coherent overall policies and plans and build appropriately on the strengths of current arrangements. (p. 7)

This chapter considers the nature of such overall policies and draws mainly upon the evolving experience within East Sussex to illustrate the issues. It should be remembered, though, that all LEAs had only a few months in which to prepare their first submission to the DES in the summer of 1986. For many the proposal was closer to an outline plan than a carefully thought out policy. More detailed statements will probably emerge as LEAs take stock and prepare for the next round. What follows, therefore, reflects current uncertainties as both the DES the local authorities and one LEA in particular pick their way through the new INSET 'maze'.

An LEA Plan for SFSD

What are the main problems facing an authority which decides to adopt and SFSD plan and involve its schools in the analysis of their own needs and the creation of policies to meet them? The following were identified in East Sussex as the SFSD project was gradually extended beyond the pilot schools.

Training — The LEA must help schools to understand what is required of them and suggest guidelines as to how they might go about preparing a policy. Training is required for those in the schools who will carry the main responsibility.

Coordination — It must devise a system which will coordinate the activities of individual schools or groups of schools within a broader framework of INSET at County and national level.

Support and evaluation — It must provide help for schools in preparing, implementing and evaluating their policies.

Financial provision — Schools will require extra resources if they are to carrry out their programmes. A budget is, therefore, needed to support both in-house and out-of-school activities.

These problems are now considered in the light of East Sussex's emerging response.

Training

The original teacher fellows were all seconded to the project for a term on a full-time basis. This time was spent in discussions at the University consulting in their own school, visiting other establishments, reading and generally preparing for the formulation of their school policy. As part of a closely knit team they became highly involved and committed and were keen to make the innovation work. The schools also received special attention in terms of regular visits from other project members, advisers and teachers from interested schools.

These opportunities could not be provided for all schools in the County; resources on that scale were simply not available. The authority, therefore, decided to initiate and evaluate a second phase of the project bringing in sixteen primary and six secondary schools and offering only a limited period of training. Those representing the twenty-two new schools would have only three days to familiarize themselves with the notion of SFSD and very little extra time, within school hours, to consult with their staff. Would this work? A successful outcome would be necessary before the extension of the scheme to all schools in the County could take place.

In the autumn term of 1986 workshops were arranged for the primary and secondary schools, each represented by a head and one other member of staff (usually a deputy head). The first two days were mainly input and discussion regarding SFSD and appraisal. Amongst the exercises undertaken by the participants in groups were:

> to establish for themselves the reasons for having a policy for SFSD; ways of analyzing needs within their own school; the main elements of a policy; the likely contents of a programme and the possible place of staff development review within an SFSD scheme. They also read and discussed the policies produced by the pilot schools.

They then returned to their own schools and began discussions with staff about preparing an SFSD policy. Several schools used an in-service day to begin the process. A number of heads, whose schools were near to each other, met several times to discuss progress and share experiences. (This suggested to the project team that a consortium approach might prove helpful as more schools entered the scheme, a point taken up again later). They all returned six weeks later for the third day of the workshop with draft policies in various stages of completion. The day was spent in small groups working through each document, raising questions and making suggestions. The resource implications of each policy were also considered. Each head took away sufficient information and ideas to begin work on the final draft which was to be completed during the following term.

Some of the schools were visited during this period by members of the project team and despite the continuing dispute over pay and conditions it was clear that good progress was being made. The teachers' associations were kept informed of plans and progress and provided their full backing.

Another development took place during this time which added to the number of schools directly involved in SFSD training. Reports were constantly being received from advisers and others in contact with schools that a growing number, having learned of the project through newsletters or personal contact, were already preparing their own policies. In order to establish how widespread this was, a questionnaire was sent to all schools in the County asking whether they already had a formal staff development policy or were thinking of devising one in the near future. It transpired that thirty schools were already engaged in the process and over 100 were considering doing so and would like assistance as soon as possible. It was, therefore, decided to provided some further training opportunities at the County's four teachers' centres. These were offered mainly to primary schools, from where most of the demand came. The short courses were spread over three evenings and covered much the same content as the three-day workshops referred to above but were in a more tightly structured form, allowing less time for discussion. About fifty schools were involved and, of these, many proceeded, without further assistance from the project team, to produce their own policies. Twenty-five of these schools later pressed to formally join the project and were invited to submit their policies along with those of the sixteen other primary schools.

When their policies were submitted to the County in the spring of 1987 they were, for the most part, well prepared and showed little sign of having been unduly influenced by the policies of the pilot schools; in the sense of merely copying them. On the basis of this evidence it was decided to proceed in the autumn of 1987 with a plan to involve all of the schools in the County.

The plan is in three parts. The first involves the remaining, thirty secondary schools and a three-day training workshop, on the lines described above, will be provided for two members of staff from each school, normally to include the head. Three general advisers, one from each of the three county areas, will also participate in these workshops in order to prepare them for their support role at the implementation stage.

Stages 2 and 3 relate to training for the primary and special schools and will take place on a 'cascade' principle over a period of two years. Stage 2 involves training the trainers. Here, it is proposed that six heads from schools already involved in the project will receive a further three days of training along with six area general advisers who will later be responsible for assisting with training and support for the remaining schools.

Three-day workshops will be provided for the remaining 200 schools during the period September 1987 and April 1989. These workshops will be led on an area basis by teams of one head and one adviser trained in stage 2 above. Two staff from each school, including the head, will be invited to participate in the workshops, which will be similar in content to those provided for secondary schools. By the summer of 1989 all schools within the County will have received training and have produced their own policies.

Coordination

If SFSD is to function effectively across the County there must be a carefully coordinated plan which incorporates the policies of each school into an overall INSET programme. It is worth recalling at this point the recommendation made following the evaluation of the seven pilot schools in chapter 2. For the schools involved, planning an SFSD programme means looking ahead for at least a year and ordering priorities. A desire to engage in many activities may have to be offset against the possible disruption caused if staff are away. The outcome may be a compromise, resulting in a finely balanced set of activities using a combination of in-school and after-school time. Schools expressed concern lest this balance be disturbed by other INSET requirements imposed upon them with only short notice. This suggests that a County INSET plan, in which proposed activities for the forthcoming year are detailed, be made available to schools early enough for them to be considered as a possible part of their annual programme.

In order to achieve this, the County opted to utilize the existing area system and the advisory service and a County Adviser for SFSD was appointed. In this way it was felt that coordination could be achieved without major changes in existing organizational structures. The general advisers, trained between January and September 1987, will have a major part to play. They will already be acquainted with what the authority would like from each school; the time scale of the exercise, the implementation strategies, the problems that might be encountered etc. It will be their job to liaise closely with the schools as the policies are formulated and implemented.

Three area advisers will each be in contact with approximately ten secondary schools. They will be responsible for coordinating activities within their area, identifying staff development needs which emerge from individual school policies and passing this information on to area INSET consultative groups. These will comprise twelve elected teacher representatives, some County Hall support staff and be chaired by a senior adviser.

Six area general advisers will liaise with primary schools in much the same way and will also report to the same area INSET committees. It is anticipated that they will require additional help in this from other advisers due to the larger number of schools involved. The special school advisers will have a similar role.

The area groups will report to the County INSET Advisory Group which will comprise senior advisers, the County

Figure 2   SFSD Structure Plan

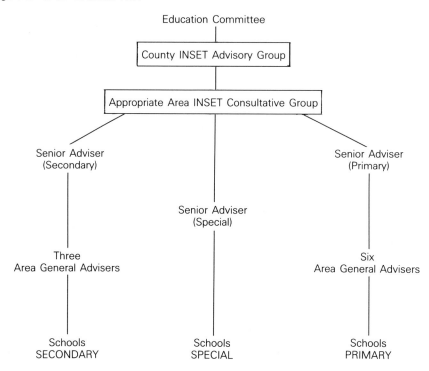

school-focussed staff development coordinator and administrative support.

The reporting structure from schools to Education Committee is shown in figure 2.

In a letter explaining the system to schools in April 1987, the County Education Officer made the following points:

> Programmes itemizing school-based activities and also those activities which might best be done on an area or County basis will be required by area general advisers on a standardized pro-forma so that they can coordinate the programmes and take recommendations identified by individual schools to the Area INSET Committee which, in turn, will pass their comments to the County INSET Planning Group. In order for these stages to take place and a County brochure to be prepared a tight timetable will be required. Nevertheless, there may be an unavoidable delay between needs being identified and any response that may be possible. But a structured programme

should enable schools to plan ahead and in consequence, reduce the disruption caused by reacting at short notice to course information.

We are here concerned with emerging plans and policies and it remains to be seen how well this system will work in practice. Hopefully, in the coming years, these structures will provide the kind of overall, forward looking planning and support that will encourage teachers and schools to take initiatives in creating programmes that will meet both individual and collective needs.

East Sussex has made considerable progress in introducing a school-focussed staff development scheme which will involve schools in assessing their own needs and producing their own policies. On the basis of this experience the coordinating structure at County level is gradually being put into place. Other LEAs may have made more progress in this respect both in setting up new INSET structures and preparing detailed INSET plans which contain lists of LEA and national courses from which schools and teachers are encouraged to choose. But the particular path chosen by East Sussex means that coordination can only be achieved in tandem with developments in the schools. For this reason each step towards a coordinating structure must be tested in the light of the increasing demands and opportunities of the SFSD scheme.

Support and Evaluation

The project has largely achieved its aims so far because it has worked with a small number of mainly self-selected schools which have shown interest and enthusiasm, for the idea of SFSD. Furthermore, these schools have received considerable attention and help from members of the project team. As the number of schools involved moves from tens to hundreds various problems may arise.

Some heads may misinterpret the nature of the task and create antagonism amongst their staff, thus inhibiting hoped-for outcomes. Some may treat it as a purely bureaucratic exercise necessary to obtain a small amount of additional money or to keep County Hall 'off their backs'. They will make all the 'right noises' but do very little. Others may be carried away by the possibilities and raise expectations for themselves and their staff which cannot possibly be fulfilled. Some might see the whole exercise as an additional burden or a waste of time and do all they can to resist.

For all of these reasons, schools will need encouragement and support. Heads and teachers will have to feel that what they are doing is not only worthwhile in itself but is also recognized as an important part of the County's INSET plan. There is little point in carefully identifying needs if these are to be ignored. There must, therefore, be people on the ground willing to listen, to explain the nature of SFSD and the part which it plays within the County INSET plan, to motivate the doubters to take part and to provide assistance in working towards school policies.

The area advisers will have a major role to play in this work. As mentioned above they will each be in contact with a group of schools and will be expected to liaise with them regarding their policies. They will be expected to offer advice on how needs for staff development within the school might be identified and ordered. They may also be asked to help with regard to the most suitable structure for administering and SFSD scheme. As programmes are formulated, they must be checked for feasibility both in terms of the ability of the school to carry them out and the availabilty of resources. For instance, problems will arise if too many staff are released too often. The head, staff development coordinator or staff development committee must ensure that activities take place at appropriate times. Disruption must be minimized if the staff development programme is not to prove counter-productive.

Schools will expect to receive some additional resources to assist with the implementation of their policies but in addition they may seek, through careful re-planning of working time or by undertaking some activities out of normal school hours, to increase the extent of their staff development programme. The experience of advisers, gained through dealing with a number of schools, will enable them to offer advice on both feasibility and resources. They should quickly spot problems which may arise if a school is over extending itself. They should also be alert to the opposite problem and may seek to encourage schools where an over cautious attitude prevails.

Advisers will also encourage schools to build into their policies suitable self-monitoring procedures. The evaluation section of an SFSD policy was considered in chapters 7 and 8. The advisers' role with respect to school self-evaluation in its broadest sense is set out in a letter to the schools from the County Education Officer.

> . . .there will be a need for schools to set up some form of self
> review in order to monitor their own progress. Outcomes

should feed back into the development plan and also inform the SFSD policy of whole school needs.

Advisers will be available to support schools' self review in various ways. For example, by cooperating by invitation in the review discussions with the staff, by providing an advisers' review report to put alongside the self review report, by providing and independent review with reports for the staff, governors and CEO or simply providing a review of one aspect of the school's activity.

The school self review should be paralled by individual staff development reviews so that individual needs and whole school needs can be harmonized through the SFSD policy for the development of both the school and the teacher which, in turn, should benefit the pupil whose improved learning experiences is the ultimate purpose of all activities.

Area advisers, clearly, have an important role to play in encouraging, supporting and monitoring the development of SFSD. Theirs will be the main responsibility but all advisers and advisory teachers will sometimes be called upon to give help and advice. Consequently, a series of two-day workshops was provided by the project team for the whole advisory service on the themes of SFSD and staff development review. The intention was to provide all advisers with sufficient knowledge to deal with requests for help of this kind.

It is also expected that schools in close proximity to each other will cooperate in two ways. The first, will involve help and support in the preparation of policies and it has already been noted that this took place naturally, without any bidding from the team, in an earlier stage of the project. The second is in connection with the more effective use of resources. It is possible that some schools may be able to work together to offer various learning opportunities for their staff through, for instance, exchanges or jointly provided workshops. The cost of an invited speaker might also be shared between two or more schools. The creation of federations of schools for these purposes will be encouraged as the main phase of training begins in late 1987.

Financial Provision

The new funding arrangements set out in Circular 6/86 have affected LEAs in a number of ways. The long established pooling system, whereby INSET monies passed in and out of a centrally administered fund, has now ceased. Part of the previously pooled resources will become available to LEAs who must, in order to obtain it, prepare their own costed plans for approval by the DES. This gives greater overall control to central government but within this framework it also provides the opportunity for each local authority to create INSET policies according to its own needs.

East Sussex is one of a number of LEAs which have granted, or are about to grant, some responsibility for planning INSET to the schools themselves, through SFSD type schemes. In these authorities, the total INSET budget, made up partly of Government contributions (50 per cent for locally assessed needs and 70 per cent for designated national priority areas) and partly from the LEA's own funds, must be allocated to cover a range of provision, including SFSD. For East Sussex this has meant that, for the first two years of the new funding arrangements, the following items have appeared in the budget.

(i)   Supply cover for training the trainers for SFSD. This represents the cost of providing the workshops as described under the heading 'training' above.

(ii) Supply cover to release the members of staff from each school for a three day workshop. This is the main cost of the training as set out above.

(iii) Travel and subsistance allowance in connection with the above.

(iv) SFSD fund against which each school will be invited to bid on the basis of one supply day per year for each member of staff. This will amount to approximately £60 per teacher although a minimum will be set to compensate the very small schools. The average sized secondary school will receive £3000 to £4000 and primary schools between £300 and £1000 on this basis.

(v)   One half a day per year, for each member of staff, for a staff development review discussion. This is a major sum which has been set aside to allow time for interviews. It is not clear at this stage whether these will take place, at least on the scale envisaged. Much depends upon the view taken by the teachers' associations and the outcome of national discussions over pay, conditions and negotiating rights.

(vi) Local INSET budget for teachers' centres. This is increased over previous years to reflect the greater part to be played by centres in the new scheme.

(vii) Staffing of INSET administration. This is necessary administrative staffing to cover the whole of INSET provision but a proportion can reasonably be attributed to SFSD due to the fact that over 400 policies must be checked and funded each year.

The total sum involved for SFSD resourcing in the first year totals something over 10 per cent of the county's INSET budget. The remainder of the county's budget is accounted for through direct and indirect expenditure on LEA-organized short courses, part-time long courses, DES courses, TVEI related in-service training (TRIST), some secondments and a number of special projects.

In future years, as the items for training for SFSD no longer apply, the proportion of the budget allocated to SFSD will be reconsidered. There will be the opportunity to increase the amount made available to schools for their own in-house activities but decisions on this issue will await further evaluation of the effects of the scheme. The amount earmarked for SFSD expenditure at present represents a not insignificant proportion of the overall INSET budget but it is still a relatively small expenditure for the amount of activity and involvement which it generates. Furthermore, it indicates a commitment on the part of the authority to support school-focussed activities and this, on the evidence of the project so far, encourages schools to seek additional ways of finding time to extend their programmes as described in earlier chapters.

And For the Future?

At present East Sussex is poised to extend SFSD to all schools in the County. The outcomes of a preliminary evaluation are given in chapter 2 and further reviews will take place as part of an overall evaluation of INSET policy set out in the county plan. Initial findings indicate that at one level the scheme has been a success and the project has achieved its aims. The representatives of the teachers' associations have backed the project and have themselves attended a workshop on SFSD and staff development review in order to become more conversant with the scheme and more able to answer questions raised by their members. Schools seem very willing to participate and there have been some outstanding examples of beneficial outcomes from creative programmes.

But as was shown in chapter 2 all schools involved have not benefited to the same extent. This is partly due to the way the scheme has been introduced in the different schools and the amount of backing it has received from the head and management team. But it has also been affected by the discontent and frustration which today afflicts many schools. It is not the intention to analyze or explain this problem here but some reference must be made to the continuing unsatisfactory state of relationships and morale within the education system, for it clearly affects the future of SFSD.

The facts are well known. Continual paring down of the education budget by central government over a decade has left the state system poorer than it was in the 1970s. At the same time there have been increasing demands made on the service both in terms of accountability or value-for-money and major curriculum and organizational changes. In many respects, too, power and direction has shifted to the centre leaving LEAs, schools and teachers feeling less in control of their own affairs. A sense that professionalism is gradually being eroded prevades and this feeling is strenghtened by the removal of traditional negotiating rights and the likelihood that new pay and conditions of service will be imposed.

The fact that SFSD has taken root in these circumstances is a credit to the dedication and perspicacity of teachers in East Sussex. But it could easily grind to a halt. If it is seen, not as a positive step towards greater professional autonomy, but as a management strategy to increase control and accountability and possibly a back door to introduce appraisal, then it will be discarded or sabotaged; and rightly so. The experience in East Sussex, however, indicates that this need not be the case. There are some positive notes on which to end and with which to look to the future.

SFSD does enable schools to play a much greater role in determining how their LEA plans and implements its INSET policy.

SFSD does enable teachers to express their own needs for staff development and to influence their school's own policy. In the process it is likely that a more coherent and extensive set of activities will emerge that will benefit the school, the teachers and the pupils.

In September 1987 the new condition of service for teachers will be implemented. How the situation will be affected by the industrial dispute it is impossible to say. What can be said, however, is that some of the conditions will both fit with and be more sensibly dealt with in the framework of an SFSD policy. The proposals refer to 195 working days of which 190 are to be devoted to teaching and other duties. The remaining five 'Baker' days are generally regarded as being for in-service activities. An SFSD policy will, surely, be essential if proper use is to be made of this time.

The DES proposals also refer to appraisal. This was discussed in chapter 5 and its relationship to staff development explained. Schools that have an ongoing staff development policy incoporating staff development review will not only be better prepared for the introduction of a formal appraisal scheme but will also be experienced enough to regard it in a positive light and as another aspect of professional development which can benefit all parties in the education process.

But all of this can easily be lost and this possibility should be heeded by the Secretary of State. Significant developments of the kind described in this book need both understanding and support from the centre. Those who have made strenuous efforts to make the scheme work will inevitably ask — will this be forthcoming?

References

Acas (1986) *Report of Working Group on Appraisal/Training* London, Advisory, Conciliation And Arbitration Service.

Acset (1983) *Making Inset Work — 1983* London, Teacher Training Sub-Committee, Advisory Committee on the Supply and Training of Teachers.

Argyris, C. and Schon, D.A. (1976) *Theory in Practice: Increasing Professional Effectiveness* San Francisco, CA, Jossey-Bass.

Baker, K. (1980) 'Planning school policies for INSET: The SITE Project' in Hoyle, E. and Megarry, J. (Eds) *World Yearbook of Education 1980 Professional Development of Teachers*, London, Kogan Page.

Baker, K. *et al* (1982) *The Schools and In-Service Teacher Evaluation Project 1979–1981*, Bristol, University of Bristol, School of Education Research Unit.

Baker, K. (1986) *LEA Responses to the New INSET Arrangements*, Education Management Exchange, Slough, NFER.

Baker, P. (1984) *Practical Self Evaluation for Teachers*, Schools Council Programme 2, York, Longmans/SCDC.

Berman, P., and McLaughan, M. (1978) *Federal Programs Supporting Educational Change, Vol VII, Factors Affecting Implementation and Continuation*, Santa Monica, CA, Rand Corporation.

Bolam, R. (Ed.) (1982) *School-Focused In-Service Training*, London, Heinemann.

Boydell, T. and Pedler, R. (1981) *Management Self-Development: Concepts and Practices*, Farnborough, Gower.

Braybrooke, D. and Lindblom, C.E. (1970) *A Strategy of Decision: Policy Evaluation as a Social Process* London, Collier MacMillan.

Butterworth, I. (1986) *The Appraisal of Teachers*, Education Management Information Exchange, Slough, NFER.

Cumbria County Council (1984) *The Appraisal and Professional Development of Teaching Staff*, Carlisle, Cumbria County Council.

Cumming, C. *et al.*, (1985) *Becoming a Better Teacher: Professional Staff Development in Scottish Secondary Schools*, Edinburgh, Moray House.

Davies, J.P. (1981) *The SITE Project in Northamptonshire 1978–1980* Northamptonshire LEA (Nene College).

DEPARTMENT OF EDUCATION AND SCIENCE (1972) *Teacher Education and Training* (The James Report), London, HMSO.

DEPARTMENT OF EDUCATION AND SCIENCE (1983) *Teaching Quality*, London, HMSO.

DEPARTMENT OF EDUCATION AND SCIENCE (1985) *Better Schools*, London, HMSO.

DEPARTMENT OF EDUCATION AND SCIENCE (1986) *Local Education Authority Training Grants Scheme: Financial Year 1987–88* Circular No 6/86, London, DES.

DEPARTMENT OF EDUCATION AND SCIENCE (1987) *School Teachers' Pay and Conditions of Employment: The Government's Proposals*, London, DES.

EASON, P. (1985) *Making School-centred INSET Work*, Course P536, Milton Keynes/Beckenham, Open University/Croom Helm.

ELLIOTT-KEMP, J. (1986) *SIGMA — a process based approach to staff development*, Sheffield City Polytechnic, PAVIC Publications.

ELLIOTT-KEMP, J. and ROGERS, C. (1982) *The Effective Teacher: A Person-Centred Development Guide.* Sheffield City Polytechnic, PAVIC Publications.

ERAUT, M. (1985) 'In-service education and training of teachers', *International Encyclopaedia of Education* pp. 2511–26.

ERAUT, M. (1986) 'Teacher appraisal and/or teacher development: Friends or foes?', *Times Educational Supplement.*

ERAUT, M. (1987) 'Evaluation and quality management', *Management in Education*, 1, 2.

FIELD, M. and MULHERN, T. (1983) 'Staff development at High Peak College: Two Viewpoints', *Quality in HE/FE: The Management of Staff Development*, Coombe Lodge Report, 15, 13. pp. 596–606.

FULLAN, M. (1982) *The Meaning of Educational Change*, Ontario, OISE Press.

FURTHER EDUCATION UNIT (1982) *Teaching Skills* London, Further Education Unit, DES.

GOODLAD, J.I. (1983) 'The school as workplace' in GRIFFIN, G.A. (Ed.) *Staff Development.* Eighty-second Yearbook of the National Society for the Study of Education, Chicago, University of Chicago Press.

GRAHAM, D. (1985) *Those Having Torches... Teacher Appraisal: A Study* Ipswich, Suffolk LEA.

HAMPSHIRE COUNTY COUNCIL (1984) *Self-Evaluation in Primary Schools*, Winchester, Hampshire County Council.

HENDERSON, E.S. (1981) 'The concept of school-focused INSET' in HENDERSON, E.S. and PERRY, G.W. (Eds) *Change and Development in Schools*, Maidenhead, McGraw-Hill.

HEWTON, E. (1986) *Education in Recession*, London, Allen and Unwin.

HMI (1982) *Report by HMI on the Effects on the Education Service in England and Wales of Local Authority Expenditure Policies — Financial Year 1981–82*, London, DES.

HMI (1985) *Quality in Schools: Evaluation and Appraisal*, London, HMSO.

HOGWOOD, B.W. and GUNN, L.A. (1984) *Policy Analysis for the Real World*, Oxford University Press.

HOYLE, E. (1972) *Innovation and the Social Organization of the School (Creativity of the School: Technical Report No 1)* Paris, OECD/CERI.

HOYLE, E. and MEGARRY, J. (Eds) (1980) *World Yearbook of Education 1980 Professional Development of Teachers*, London, Kogan Page.

ILEA (1977) *Keeping the School Under Review*, London, ILEA Learning Material Centre.

JAMES, C. and NEWMAN, J. (1985) 'Staff appraisal: current practice in schools', *Contributions*, No 8, York, Centre for the Study of Comprehensive Schools, pp. 23–30.

JAMES, M. (1982) *A First Review and Register of School and College Initiated Self-evaluation Activities in the United Kingdom*, Milton Keynes, Education Faculty, Open University.

JENKINS, W.I. (1978) *Policy Analysis: A Political Perspective*, London, Martin Robertson.

LONG, P. (1986) *Performance Appraisal Revisited*, Third IPM survey, London, Institute of Personnel Management.

McCORMICK, R. and JAMES, M. (1983) *Curriculum Evaluation in Schools*, Beckenham, Croom Helm.

MacGREGOR BURNS, J. (1978) *Leadership*, London, Harper Row.

McMAHON, A., BOLAM, R., ABBOTT, R. and HOLLY, P. (1984) *Guidelines for Review and Development in Schools*, Primary School Handbook (secondary handbook also available), York, Longmans/SCDC.

MORANT, W.R. (1981) *In-Service Education within the School*, London, Allen and Unwin.

MYERS, M. (1987) *System Supplied Information*. A programme of assessing staff development needs in schools, Birmingham, Faculty of Education, University of Birmingham.

NAISMITH, D. (1985) *Proposals for a System of Professional Performance Appraisal*, Croydon, Croydon Education Authority.

NORTHAMPTONSHIRE LEA (1984) *School Focused In-Service Education* Northampton, Northamptonshire Education Department.

NOTTINGHAMSHIRE COUNTY COUNCIL (1983) *Teacher Professional Appraisal as Part of a Development Programme*, Nottinghamshire, Nottinghamshire County Council Education Department, Advisory and Inspection Service.

NUTTALL, D.L. (1985) *School Self-Evaluation. Accountability with a Human Face*, York, Longmans/SCDC.

OLDROYD, D., SMITH, K. and LEE, J. (1984) *School-based Staff Development Activities. A Handbook for Secondary Schools*, Schools Council Programme 1, York, Longmans.

OPEN UNIVERSITY (1981) *Curriculum in Action: An Approach to Evaluation*, Course P234 Milton Keynes, Open University Press.

OPEN UNIVERSITY (1982) *Course E364: Curriculum Evaluation and Assessment in Educational Institutions*, Milton Keynes, Open University Press.

PARLETT, M. and HAMILTON, D. (1981) 'Evaluation as illumination' in PARLETT, M. and DEARDEN, G. (Eds) *Introduction to Illuminative Evaluation*, Guildford, Society for Research into Higher Education.

PERRY, P. (1977) from a keynote address to *OECD/CERI International Workshop on School-Focussed INSET*, Florida, November.

RANDELL, G., PACKARD, P. and SLATER, J. (1984) *Staff Appraisal*, London, Institute of Personnel Management.

SARASON, S.B. (1982) *The Culture of the School and the Problem of Change*, 2nd edn, Boston, Allyn and Bacon.

SHIPMAN, M. (1983) *In-school Evaluation*, London, Heinemann.

TAMSETT, R. (1982) 'Study 4: Teacher-teacher partnerships in the observation of classrooms' in RUDDUCK, J. (Ed.) *Teachers in Partnership: Four Studies of In-service Collaboration*, York, Longmans/SCDC.

TRETHOWAN D. (1983) *Target Setting*, London, Education for Industrial Society.

TRETHOWAN D. (1986) 'Target setting and appraisal at Warden Park School' in DAY, C. and MOORE, R. (Eds) *Staff Development in the Secondary School*, Beckenham, Croom Helm.

TURNER, G. and CLIFT, P. (1985) *A First Review and Register of School Based Teacher Appraisal Schemes*, Milton Keynes, School of Education, Open University.

WARWICK, D. (1983) *Staff Appraisal*, London, Education for Industrial Society.

WOODCOCK, M. and FRANCIS, D. (1982) *The Unblocked Manager: A Practical Guide to Self-development*, Aldershot, Gower.

Index